# Connecting Networks Lab Manual

Cisco Networking Academy

CISCO

Cisco Press
800 East 96th Street
Indianapolis, Indiana 46240

Connecting Networks Lab Manual
Cisco Networking Academy



Published by:
Cisco Press
800 East 96th Street
Indianapolis, IN 46240 USA



Printed in the United States of America

First Printing December 2013

ISBN-13: 9781587133312

ISBN-10: 1587133318

## Warning and Disclaimer

This book is designed to provide information about Connecting Networks. Every effort has been made to make this book as complete and as accurate as possible, but no warranty or fitness is implied.

The information is provided on an "as is" basis. The authors, Cisco Press, and Cisco Systems, Inc. shall have neither liability nor responsibility to any person or entity with respect to any loss or damages arising from the information contained in this book or from the use of the discs or programs that may accompany it.

The opinions expressed in this book belong to the author and are not necessarily those of Cisco Systems, Inc.

## Trademark Acknowledgments

All terms mentioned in this book that are known to be trademarks or service marks have been appropriately capitalized. Cisco Press or Cisco Systems, Inc., cannot attest to the accuracy of this information. Use of a term in this book should not be regarded as affecting the validity of any trademark or service mark.

This book is part of the Cisco Networking Academy® series from Cisco Press. The products in this series support and complement the Cisco Networking Academy curriculum. If you are using this book outside the Networking Academy, then you are not preparing with a Cisco trained and authorized Networking Academy provider.

CISCO

For more information on the Cisco Networking Academy or to locate a Networking Academy, please visit www.cisco.com/edu.

# Feedback Information

At Cisco Press, our goal is to create in-depth technical books of the highest quality and value. Each book is crafted with care and precision, undergoing rigorous development that involves the unique expertise of members from the professional technical community.

Readers' feedback is a natural continuation of this process. If you have any comments regarding how we could improve the quality of this book, or otherwise alter it to better suit your needs, you can contact us through email at feedback@ciscopress.com. Please make sure to include the book title and ISBN in your message.

We greatly appreciate your assistance.


| | |
|---|---|
| **Publisher** | **Paul Boger** |
| **Associate Publisher** | **Dave Dusthimer** |
| **Business Operations Manager, Cisco Press** | **Jan Cornelssen** |
| **Executive Editor** | **Mary Beth Ray** |
| **Managing Editor** | **Sandra Schroeder** |
| **Project Editor** | **Seth Kerney** |
| **Editorial Assistant** | **Vanessa Evans** |
| **Cover Designer** | **Mark Shirar** |
| **Compositor** | **TnT Design, Inc.** |


---

**Americas Headquarters**
Cisco Systems, Inc.
San Jose, CA

**Asia Pacific Headquarters**
Cisco Systems (USA) Pte. Ltd.
Singapore

**Europe Headquarters**
Cisco Systems International BV
Amsterdam, The Netherlands

Cisco has more than 200 offices worldwide. Addresses, phone numbers, and fax numbers are listed on the Cisco Website at **www.cisco.com/go/offices.**

# Contents


**Chapter 1 — Hierarchical Network Design** .......... **1**

1.0.1.2 Class Activity – Design Hierarchy .......... 1

1.4.1.1 Class Activity – Borderless Innovations – Everywhere .......... 2

**Chapter 2 — Connecting to the WAN** .......... **3**

2.0.1.2 Class Activity – Branching Out .......... 3

2.2.4.3 Lab – Researching WAN Technologies .......... 5

2.3.1.1 Class Activity – WAN Device Modules .......... 10

**Chapter 3 — Point-to-Point Connections** .......... **11**

3.0.1.2 Class Activity – PPP Persuasion .......... 11

3.3.2.8 Lab – Configuring Basic PPP with Authentication .......... 12

3.4.1.5 Lab – Troubleshooting Basic PPP with Authentication .......... 29

3.5.1.1 Class Activity – PPP Validation .......... 37

**Chapter 4 — Frame Relay** .......... **39**

4.0.1.2 Class Activity – Emerging WAN Technologies .......... 39

4.2.2.7 Lab – Configuring Frame Relay and Subinterfaces .......... 40

4.3.1.6 Lab – Troubleshooting Basic Frame Relay .......... 58

4.4.1.1 Class Activity – Frame Relay Budget Proposal .......... 64

**Chapter 5 — Network Address Translation for IPv4** .......... **65**

5.0.1.2 Class Activity – Conceptual NAT .......... 65

5.2.2.6 Lab – Configuring Dynamic and Static NAT .......... 66

5.2.3.7 Lab – Configuring Port Address Translation (PAT) .......... 75

5.3.1.5 Lab – Troubleshooting NAT Configurations .......... 81

5.4.1.1 Class Activity – NAT Check .......... 86

**Chapter 6 — Broadband Solutions** .......... **87**

6.0.1.2 Class Activity – Broadband Varieties .......... 87

6.2.4.2 Lab – Researching Broadband Internet Access Technologies .......... 88

6.3.2.3 Lab – Configuring a Router as a PPPoE Client for DSL Connectivity .......... 93

6.4.1.1 Class Activity – Telework Proposal .......... 98

**Chapter 7 — Securing Site-to-Site Connectivity** **99**
7.0.1.2 Class Activity – VPNs at a Glance 99
7.2.2.5 Lab – Configuring a Point-to-Point GRE VPN Tunnel 100
7.5.1.1 Class Activity – VPN Planning Design 106
**Chapter 8 — Monitoring the Network** **107**
8.0.1.2 Class Activity – Network Maintenance Development 107
8.1.2.6 Lab – Configuring Syslog and NTP 108
8.2.1.8 Lab – Researching Network Monitoring Software 116
8.2.2.4 Lab – Configuring SNMP 119
8.3.3.3 Lab – Collecting and Analyzing NetFlow Data 129
8.4.1.1 Class Activity – A Network Administrator's Toolbox for Monitoring 136
**Chapter 9 — Troubleshooting the Network** **137**
9.0.1.2 Class Activity – Network Breakdown 137
9.3.1.1 Class Activity – Documentation Development 138

## About This Lab Manual

*Connecting Networks Lab Manual* contains all the labs and class activities from the Cisco Networking Academy course of the same name. It is meant to be used within this program of study.

## More Practice

If you would like more practice activities, combine your Lab Manual with the new *CCNA Routing and Switching Practice and Study Guide* ISBN: 9781587133442

## Other Related Titles

*CCNA Routing and Switching Portable Command Guide* ISBN: 9781587204302 (or eBook ISBN: 9780133381368)

*Connecting Networks Companion Guide* ISBN: 9781587133329 (or eBook ISBN: 9780133476521)

*Connecting Networks Course Booklet* ISBN: 9781587133305

## Command Syntax Conventions

The conventions used to present command syntax in this book are the same conventions used in the IOS Command Reference. The Command Reference describes these conventions as follows:

- **Boldface** indicates commands and keywords that are entered literally as shown. In actual configuration examples and output (not general command syntax), boldface indicates commands that are manually input by the user (such as a **show** command).
- *Italic* indicates arguments for which you supply actual values.
- Vertical bars (|) separate alternative, mutually exclusive elements.
- Square brackets ([ ]) indicate an optional element.
- Braces ({ }) indicate a required choice.
- Braces within brackets ([{ }]) indicate a required choice within an optional element.

# Chapter 1 — Hierarchical Network Design

## 1.0.1.2 Class Activity – Design Hierarchy

### Objective

Identify the three layers of a hierarchical network and how they are used in network design.

### Scenario

A network administrator is tasked with designing an expanded network for the company.

After speaking with network administrators in other branches of the company, it was decided to use the Cisco three-layer hierarchical network design model to guide the expansion. This model was chosen for its simple influence upon network planning.

The three layers of the expanded network design include:

- Access
- Distribution
- Core

### Resources

- World Wide Web access
- Presentation software

#### Step 1: Use the Internet to research the Cisco three-layer design model for images only.

a. Find two images that show the three-layer hierarchical design model.

b. Note the online image's web address.

#### Step 2: Study the two images you have selected from Step 1.

a. Notice the types of equipment in each layer of the designs you have chosen.

b. Differentiate why it is assumed the types of equipment shown in the images are located where they are on the design.

c. Notice any other differences between the chosen images.

1) Number of devices used within the layers

2) Redundancy, if any

#### Step 3: Create a three-slide presentation to include:

a. The two chosen designs with hyperlinks as to their Internet site locations.

b. A statement on each slide as to why the particular image was chosen.

c. Comparison statements as to how the two images differ, but with an explanation of why they are classified as three-level hierarchical designs.

#### Step 4: Present the slides to a classmate, another group, or the class for discussion.

# 1.4.1.1 Class Activity – Borderless Innovations – Everywhere

## Objective

Describe borderless networks components.

## Scenario

You are the network administrator for your small- to medium-sized business. Borderless network services interest you as you plan your network's future.

While planning for network policies and services, you realize that your wired and wireless networks need manageability and deployment design.

Therefore, this leads you to consider the following Cisco borderless services as possible options for your business:

- Security – ***TrustSec***
- Mobility – ***Motion***
- Application Performance – ***App Velocity***
- Multimedia Performance – ***Medianet***
- Energy Management – ***EnergyWise***

## Resources

- World Wide Web access
- Word processing or presentation software

## Directions

### Step 1: Select three Cisco borderless network services that interest you from the following list:

- Security – ***TrustSec***
- Mobility – ***Motion***
- Application performance – ***App Velocity***
- Multimedia performance – ***Medianet***
- Energy management – ***EnergyWise***

### Step 2: Using the Internet, research your three selections. Consider finding short video presentations and various websites of the three borderless network services you selected. Be sure to take notes on your research:

a. Based on your research, create a basic definition of each borderless network service.

b. List at least three areas of assistance each borderless service offers to network administrators.

### Step 3: Prepare an informational matrix listing the three borderless network services you selected. Include the video notes you completed in Steps 2a and b.

### Step 4: Share your matrix with another student, group, or the entire class.

# Chapter 2 — Connecting to the WAN

## 2.0.1.2 Class Activity – Branching Out

### Objective

Describe WAN access technologies available to small-to-medium-sized business networks.

### Scenario

Your medium-sized company is opening a new branch office to serve a wider, client-based network. This branch will focus on regular, day-to-day network operations, but will also provide TelePresence, web conferencing, IP telephony, video on demand, and wireless services.

Although you know that an ISP can provide WAN routers and switches to accommodate the branch office connectivity for the network, you prefer to use your own customer premises equipment (CPE). To ensure interoperability, Cisco devices have been used in all other branch-office WANs.

As the branch-office network administrator, it is your responsibility to research possible network devices for purchase and use over the WAN.

### Resources

- World Wide Web
- Word processing software

### Directions

**Step 1: Visit the Cisco Branch-WAN Business Calculator site. Accept the agreement to use the calculator.**

**Step 2: Input information to help the calculator determine a preferred router or ISR option for your branch and WAN (both).**

**Note**: There is a slider tool within the calculator window that allows the choice of more service options for your branch office and WAN.

**Step 3: The calculator will suggest a possible router or ISR device solution for your branch office and WAN. Use the tabs at the top of the calculator window to view the output.**

**Step 4: Create a matrix with three column headings and list some information provided by the output in each category:**

- Return on investment (ROI)
- Total cost of ownership (TCO)
- Energy savings

**Step 5: Discuss your research with a classmate, group, class, or your instructor. Include in your discussion:**

- Specifics on the requirements of your network as used for calculator input
- Output information from your matrix
- Additional factors you would consider before purchasing a router or ISR for your new branch office

# 2.2.4.3 Lab – Researching WAN Technologies

## Objectives

**Part 1: Investigate Dedicated WAN Technologies and Providers**

**Part 2: Investigate a Dedicated Leased Line Service Provider in Your Area**

## Background / Scenario

Today's broadband Internet services are fast, affordable, and secure using VPN technologies. However, many companies still find the need for a 24-hour dedicated connection to the Internet or a dedicated point-to-point connection from one office location to another. In this lab, you will investigate the cost and availability of purchasing a dedicated T1 Internet connection for your home or business.

## Required Resources

Device with Internet access

## Part 1: Investigate Dedicated WAN Technologies and Providers

In Part 1, you will research basic characteristics of dedicated WAN technologies, and in Step 2, you will discover providers that offer dedicated WAN services.

### Step 1: Research WAN technology characteristics.

Use search engines and websites to research the following WAN technologies to complete the table below.

| WAN Technology | Dedicated Connection (yes/no) | Last Mile Media | | | Speed/Range |
|---|---|---|---|---|---|
| | | Copper (yes/no) | Fiber (yes/no) | Wireless (yes/no) | |
| T1/DS1 | | | | | |
| T3/DS3 | | | | | |
| OC3 (SONET) | | | | | |
| Frame Relay | | | | | |
| ATM | | | | | |
| MPLS | | | | | |
| EPL (Ethernet Private Line) | | | | | |

### Step 2: Discover dedicated WAN technology service providers.

Navigate to http://www.telarus.com/carriers.html. This webpage lists the Internet service providers (also known as carriers) that partner with Telarus to provide automated real-time telecom pricing. Click the links to the various carrier partners and search for the dedicated WAN technologies that they provide. Complete the table below by identifying each service provider's dedicated WAN services, based on the information provided on the website. Use the extra lines provided in the table to record additional service providers.

| Internet Service Provider | T1/DS1/PRI | T3/DS3 | OC3 (SONET) | Frame Relay | ATM | MPLS | EPL Ethernet Private Line |
|---|---|---|---|---|---|---|---|
| Comcast | | | | | | | x |
| Integra | x | x | x | | | x | x |
| tw telecom | | x | x | | | x | |
| AT&T | | | | | | | |
| Cbeyond | | | | | | | |
| Earthlink | | | | | | | |
| Level 3 Communications | | | | | | | |
| XO Communications | | | | | | | |
| Verizon | | | | | | | |
| | | | | | | | |
| | | | | | | | |
| | | | | | | | |

## Part 2: Investigate a Dedicated Leased Line Service Provider in Your Area

In Part 2, you will research a local service provider that will provide a T1 dedicated leased line to the geographical area specified. This application requires a name, address, and phone number before the search can be performed. You may wish to use your current information or research an address locally where a business might be looking for a WAN connection.

### Step 1: Navigate to http://www.telarus.com/geoquote.html to try GeoQuote.

GeoQuote is a web application that automates the search for WAN technology service providers, and provides price quotes in real-time. Fill in the required fields.

a. Click the **Service Type** drop-down list and select **Data (High Speed Internet)**.

b. Type your **First Name** and **Last Name**, your sample **Company**, and your **Email** address.

c. Type the **Phone Number** to connect to the WAN. This number should be a landline number.

d. Click the button marked **Step 2**.

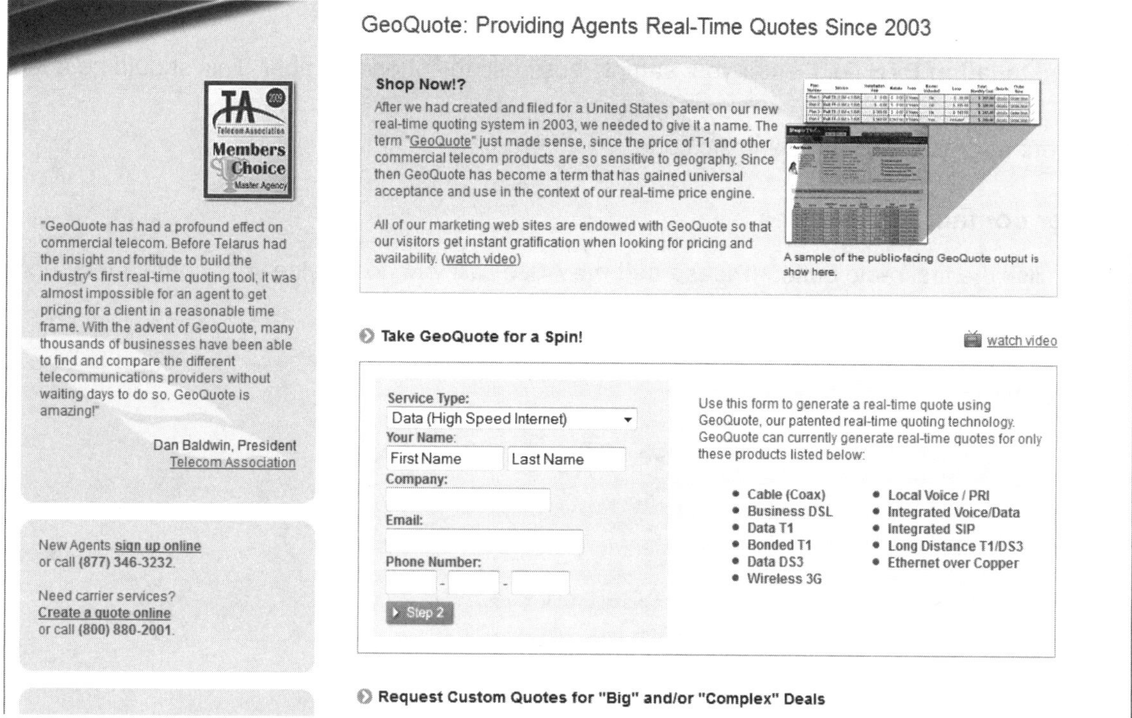


## Step 2: Select the service type.

Choose **Internet T1 (1.5 MB)** and scroll down to **Step 3** on the webpage.

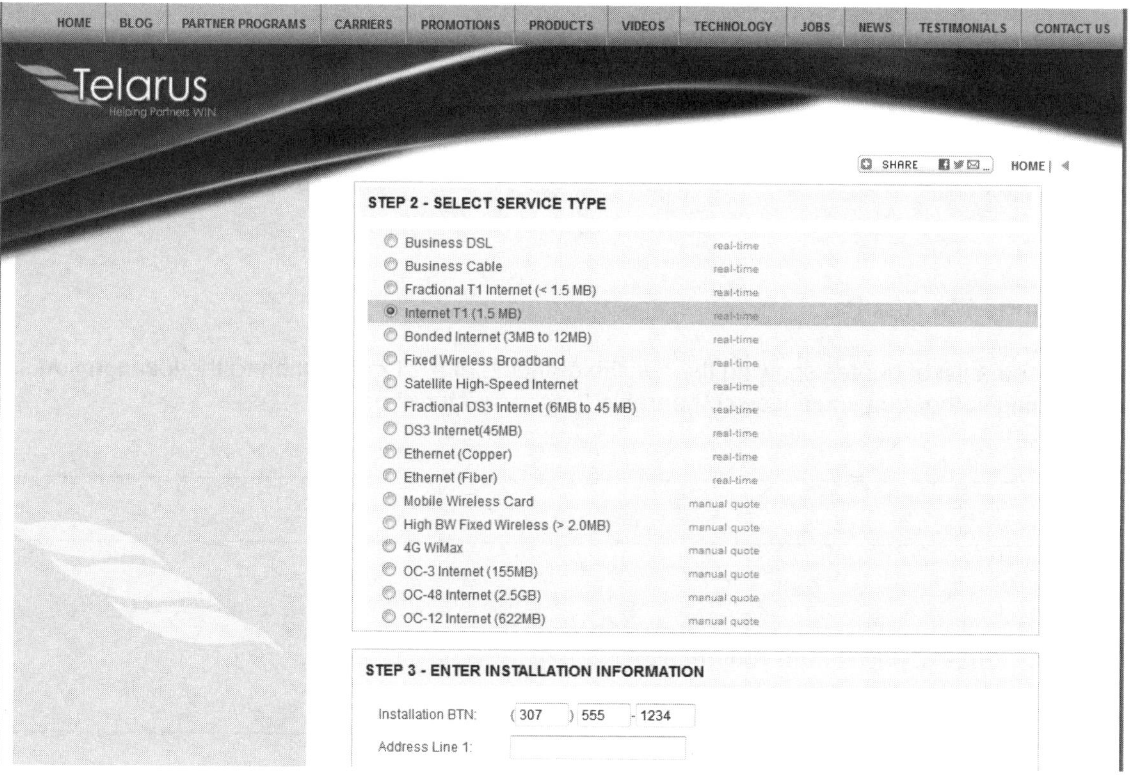

## Step 3: Enter installation information.

a. In the **Installation BTN** field, enter your sample business telephone number. This should be a landline number.

b. Enter your address, city, state, and zip code.

## Step 4: Enter contact preferences.

a. Do not click the first radio button (**Please call me ASAP at**), but do provide your contact telephone number.

b. Click the **I am just window shopping** radio button.

c. Click **Continue**.

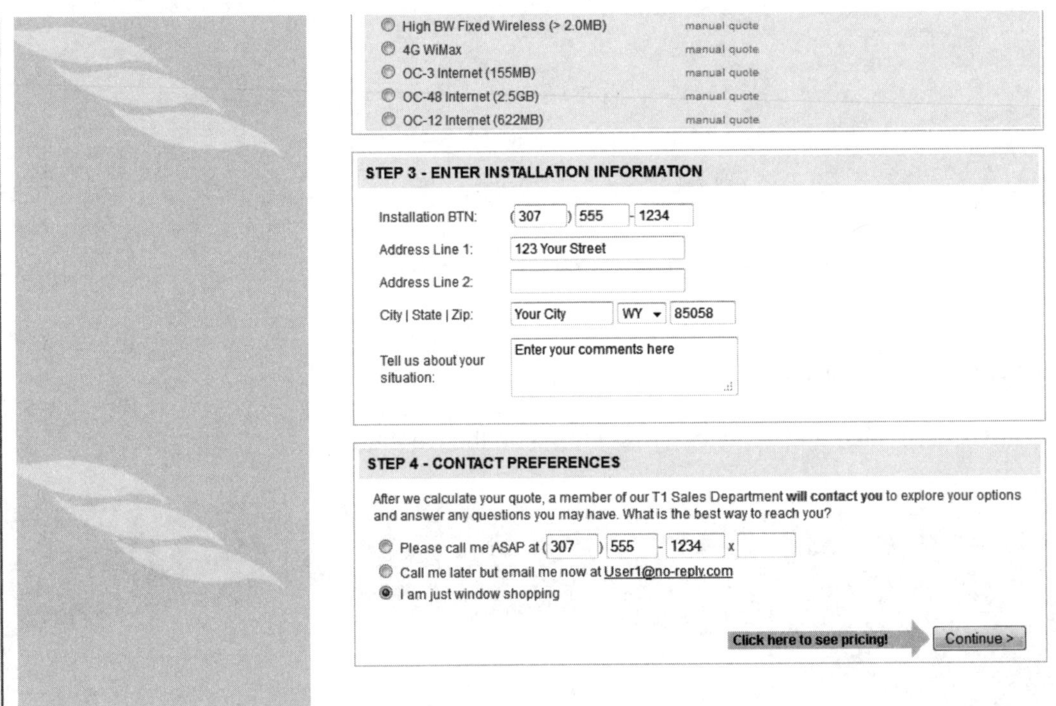


## Step 5: Examine the results.

You should see a list of quotes showing the available pricing of a T1 connection to the location you specified. Was the pricing in the area you chose comparable to those pictured below?

_______________________________________________

_______________________________________________

What was the range of prices from your results?

_______________________________________________

_______________________________________________

| | Plan | Service Type | Bandwidth | Install | Rebate | Term | Router | Loop | Monthly Cost ↓ | Order |
|---|---|---|---|---|---|---|---|---|---|---|
| | 1 | Internet T1 (1.5 MB) | 1.5M x 1.5M | $0.00 | $0.00 | 3 Year | No | $35.33 | $210.33 | Order Now |
| | 2 | Internet T1 (1.5 MB) | 1.5M x 1.5M | $0.00 | $0.00 | 3 Year | No | $128.51 | $229.91 | Order Now |
| | 3 | Internet T1 (1.5 MB) | 1.5M x 1.5M | $0.00 | $0.00 | 2 Year | No | $46.67 | $231.67 | Order Now |
| | 4 | Internet T1 (1.5 MB) | 1.5M x 1.5M | $345.87 | $0.00 | 5 Year | No | $117.13 | $246.73 | Order Now |
| | 5 | Internet T1 (1.5 MB) | 1.5M x 1.5M | $345.87 | $0.00 | 3 Year | No | $117.13 | $254.83 | Order Now |
| | 6 | Internet T1 (1.5 MB) | 1.5M x 1.5M | $0.00 | $0.00 | 3 Year | No | $202.02 | $256.62 | Order Now |
| | 7 | Internet T1 (1.5 MB) | 1.5M x 1.5M | $345.87 | $0.00 | 2 Year | No | $117.13 | $262.93 | Order Now |
| | 8 | Internet T1 (1.5 MB) | 1.5M x 1.5M | $0.00 | $0.00 | 1 Year | No | $58.01 | $268.01 | Order Now |
| | 9 | Internet T1 (1.5 MB) | 1.5M x 1.5M | $345.87 | $0.00 | 1 Year | No | $117.13 | $279.13 | Order Now |
| | 10 | Internet T1 (1.5 MB) | 1.5M x 1.5M | $50.00 | $0.00 | 3 Year | Yes | $70.33 | $280.33 | Order Now |
| | 11 | Internet T1 (1.5 MB) | 1.5M x 1.5M | $0.00 | $0.00 | 3 Year | Yes | $202.02 | $285.62 | Order Now |
| | 12 | Internet T1 (1.5 MB) | 1.5M x 1.5M | $0.00 | $0.00 | 3 Year | Yes | included | $288.00 | Order Now |
| | 13 | Internet T1 (1.5 MB) | 1.5M x 1.5M | $0.00 | $0.00 | 3 Year | No | included | $299.00 | Order Now |
| | 14 | Internet T1 (1.5 MB) | 1.5M x 1.5M | $50.00 | $0.00 | 2 Year | Yes | $81.67 | $301.67 | Order Now |
| | 15 | Internet T1 (1.5 MB) | 1.5M x 1.5M | $0.00 | $0.00 | 3 Year | Yes | $146.00 | $306.00 | Order Now |
| | 16 | Internet T1 (1.5 MB) | 1.5M x 1.5M | $0.00 | $0.00 | 3 Year | Yes | included | $318.00 | Order Now |

## Reflection

1. What are the disadvantages to using a T1 leased line for personal home use? What would be a better solution?

_______________________________________________

2. When might the use of a dedicated WAN connection, of any type, be a good connectivity solution for a business.

_______________________________________________

3. Describe other WAN technologies that provide high-speed, low-cost options that could be an alternative solution to a T1 connection.

_______________________________________________

# 2.3.1.1 Class Activity – WAN Device Modules

## Objective

Select WAN access technologies to satisfy business requirements in a small-to-medium-sized business network.

## Scenario

Your medium-sized company is upgrading its network. To make the most of the equipment currently in use, you decide to purchase WAN modules instead of new equipment.

All branch offices use either Cisco 1900 or 2911 series ISRs. You will be updating these routers in several locations. Each branch has its own ISP requirements to consider.

To update the devices, focus on the following WAN modules access types:

- Ethernet
- Broadband
- T1/E1 and ISDN PRI
- BRI
- Serial
- T1 and E1 Trunk Voice and WAN
- Wireless LANs and WANs

## Resources

- World Wide Web
- Word processing software

## Directions

**Step 1: Visit Interfaces and Modules. On this page, you will see many options ISR interface modules options – remember that you currently own and use only the Cisco 1900 and 2900 series routers.**

**Note:** If the above link is no longer valid, search the Cisco site for "Interfaces and Modules".

**Step 2: Create a comparison matrix listing the following WAN access types for your branch networks:**

- Ethernet
- Broadband
- T1/E1 and ISDN PRI
- BRI
- Serial WAN
- T1 and E1Trunk Voice and WAN
- Wireless LANs and WANs

**Step 3: In the matrix, record the interface module type you need to purchase for your ISRs for upgrade purposes.**

**Step 4: Use the Internet to research pictures of the modules. Provide a screenshot of the module or a hyperlink to a picture of each module.**

**Step 5: Share your matrix with a classmate, group, class, or your instructor.**

# Chapter 3 — Point-to-Point Connections

## 3.0.1.2 Class Activity – PPP Persuasion

### Objectives

Describe the benefits of using PPP over HDLC in a WAN.

### Scenario

Your network engineering supervisor recently attended a networking conference where Layer 2 protocols were discussed. He knows that you have Cisco equipment on the premises, but he would also like to offer security and advanced TCP/IP options and controls on that same equipment by using the Point-to-Point Protocol (PPP).

After researching the PPP protocol, you find it offers some advantages over the HDLC protocol, currently used on your network.

Create a matrix listing the advantages and disadvantages of using the HDLC vs. PPP protocols. When comparing the two protocols, include:

- Ease of configuration
- Adaptability to non-proprietary network equipment
- Security options
- Bandwidth usage and compression
- Bandwidth consolidation

Share your chart with another student or class. Justify whether or not you would suggest sharing the matrix with the network engineering supervisor to justify a change being made from HDLC to PPP for Layer 2 network connectivity.

### Resources

- Internet access to the World Wide Web
- Word processing or spreadsheet software

# 3.3.2.8 Lab – Configuring Basic PPP with Authentication

## Topology

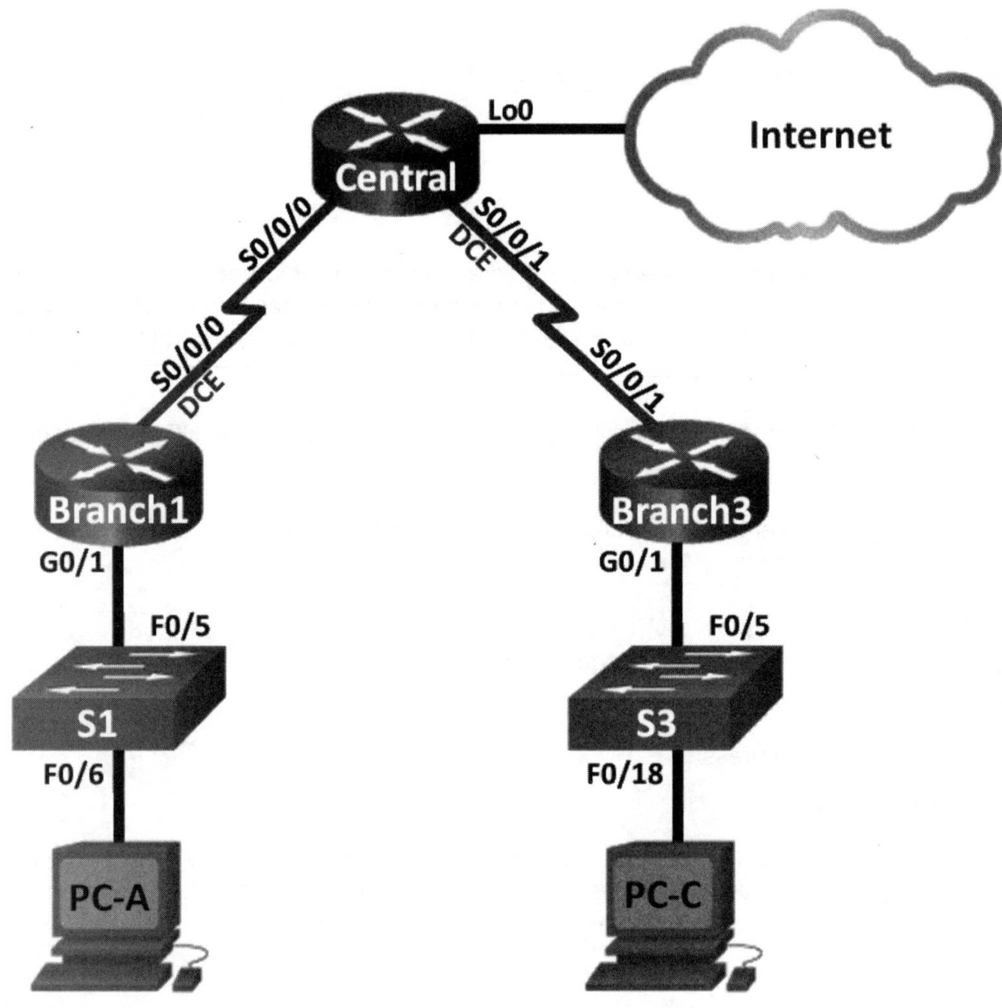


## Addressing Table

| Device | Interface | IP Address | Subnet Mask | Default Gateway |
|---|---|---|---|---|
| Branch1 | G0/1 | 192.168.1.1 | 255.255.255.0 | N/A |
| | S0/0/0 (DCE) | 10.1.1.1 | 255.255.255.252 | N/A |
| Central | S0/0/0 | 10.1.1.2 | 255.255.255.252 | N/A |
| | S0/0/1 (DCE) | 10.2.2.2 | 255.255.255.252 | N/A |
| | Lo0 | 209.165.200.225 | 255.255.255.224 | N/A |
| Branch3 | G0/1 | 192.168.3.1 | 255.255.255.0 | N/A |
| | S0/0/1 | 10.2.2.1 | 255.255.255.252 | N/A |
| PC-A | NIC | 192.168.1.3 | 255.255.255.0 | 192.168.1.1 |
| PC-C | NIC | 192.168.3.3 | 255.255.255.0 | 192.168.3.1 |

## Objectives

**Part 1: Configure Basic Device Settings**

**Part 2: Configure PPP Encapsulation**

**Part 3: Configure PPP CHAP Authentication**

## Background / Scenario

The Point-to-Point Protocol (PPP) is a very common Layer 2 WAN protocol. PPP can be used to connect from LANs to service provider WANs and for connection of LAN segments within an enterprise network.

In this lab, you will configure PPP encapsulation on dedicated serial links between the branch routers and a central router. You will configure PPP Challenge Handshake Authentication Protocol (CHAP) on the PPP serial links. You will also examine the effects of the encapsulation and authentication changes on the status of the serial link.

**Note**: The routers used with CCNA hands-on labs are Cisco 1941 Integrated Services Routers (ISRs) with Cisco IOS Release 15.2(4)M3 (universalk9 image). The switches used are Cisco Catalyst 2960s with Cisco IOS Release 15.0(2) (lanbasek9 image). Other routers, switches, and Cisco IOS versions can be used. Depending on the model and Cisco IOS version, the commands available and output produced might vary from what is shown in the labs. Refer to the Router Interface Summary Table at the end of this lab for the correct interface identifiers.

**Note**: Make sure that the routers and switches have been erased and have no startup configurations. If you are unsure, contact your instructor.

## Required Resources

- 3 Routers (Cisco 1941 with Cisco IOS Release 15.2(4)M3 universal image or comparable)
- 2 Switches (Cisco 2960 with Cisco IOS Release 15.0(2) lanbasek9 image or comparable)
- 2 PCs (Windows 7, Vista, or XP with terminal emulation program, such as Tera Term)
- Console cables to configure the Cisco IOS devices via the console ports
- Ethernet and serial cables as shown in the topology

## Part 1: Configure Basic Device Settings

In Part 1, you will set up the network topology and configure basic router settings, such as the interface IP addresses, routing, device access, and passwords.

### Step 1: Cable the network as shown in the topology.

Attach the devices as shown in the Topology, and cable as necessary.

### Step 2: Initialize and reload the routers and switches.

### Step 3: Configure basic settings for each router.

a. Disable DNS lookup.
b. Configure the device name.
c. Encrypt plain text passwords.
d. Create a message of the day (MOTD) banner warning users that unauthorized access is prohibited.
e. Assign **class** as the encrypted privileged EXEC mode password.
f. Assign **cisco** as the console and vty password and enable login.
g. Set console logging to synchronous mode.
h. Apply the IP addresses to Serial and Gigabit Ethernet interfaces according to the Addressing Table and activate the physical interfaces.
i. Set the clock rate to **128000** for DCE serial interfaces.
j. Create **Loopback0** on the Central router to simulate access to the Internet and assign an IP address according to the Addressing Table.

### Step 4: Configure routing.

a. Enable single-area OSPF on the routers and use a process ID of 1. Add all the networks, except 209.165.200.224/27 into the OSPF process.
b. Configure a default route to the simulated Internet on the Central router using Lo0 as the exit interface and redistribute this route into the OSPF process.
c. Issue the **show ip route ospf**, **show ip ospf interface brief**, and **show ip ospf neighbor** commands on all routers to verify that OSPF is configured correctly. Take note of the router ID for each router.

### Step 5: Configure the PCs.

Assign IP addresses and default gateways to the PCs according to the Addressing Table.

### Step 6: Verify end-to-end connectivity.

All devices should be able to ping other devices in the Topology. If not, troubleshoot until you can establish end-to-end connectivity.

**Note**: It may be necessary to disable the PC firewall to ping between PCs.

### Step 7: Save your configurations.

# Part 2: Configure PPP Encapsulation

## Step 1: Display the default serial encapsulation.

On the routers, issue **show interfaces serial** *interface-id* to display the current serial encapsulation.

```
Branch1# show interfaces s0/0/0
Serial0/0/0 is up, line protocol is up
  Hardware is WIC MBRD Serial
  Internet address is 10.1.1.1/30
  MTU 1500 bytes, BW 1544 Kbit/sec, DLY 20000 usec,
     reliability 255/255, txload 1/255, rxload 1/255
  Encapsulation HDLC, loopback not set
  Keepalive set (10 sec)
  Last input 00:00:02, output 00:00:05, output hang never
  Last clearing of "show interface" counters never
  Input queue: 0/75/0/0 (size/max/drops/flushes); Total output drops: 0
  Queueing strategy: fifo
  Output queue: 0/40 (size/max)
  5 minute input rate 0 bits/sec, 0 packets/sec
  5 minute output rate 0 bits/sec, 0 packets/sec
     1003 packets input, 78348 bytes, 0 no buffer
     Received 527 broadcasts (0 IP multicasts)
     0 runts, 0 giants, 0 throttles
     0 input errors, 0 CRC, 0 frame, 0 overrun, 0 ignored, 0 abort
     1090 packets output, 80262 bytes, 0 underruns
     0 output errors, 0 collisions, 3 interface resets
     0 unknown protocol drops
     0 output buffer failures, 0 output buffers swapped out
     2 carrier transitions
     DCD=up  DSR=up  DTR=up  RTS=up  CTS=up
```

What is the default serial encapsulation for a Cisco router? ____________________

## Step 2: Change the serial encapsulation to PPP.

a. Issue the **encapsulation ppp** command on the S0/0/0 interface for the Branch1 router to change the encapsulation from HDLC to PPP.

```
Branch1(config)# interface s0/0/0
Branch1(config-if)# encapsulation ppp
Branch1(config-if)#
Jun 19 06:02:33.687: %OSPF-5-ADJCHG: Process 1, Nbr 209.165.200.225 on Serial0/0/0
from FULL to DOWN, Neighbor Down: Interface down or detached
Branch1(config-if)#
Jun 19 06:02:35.687: %LINEPROTO-5-UPDOWN: Line protocol on Interface Serial0/0/0,
changed state to down
```

b. Issue the command to display the line status and line protocol for interface S0/0/0 on the Branch1 router. Document the command issued. What is current interface status for S0/0/0?

____________________________________________________________

c. Issue the **encapsulation ppp** command on interface S0/0/0 for the Central router to correct the serial encapsulation mismatch.

```
Central(config)# interface s0/0/0
Central(config-if)# encapsulation ppp
Central(config-if)#
.Jun 19 06:03:41.186: %LINEPROTO-5-UPDOWN: Line protocol on Interface Serial0/0/0, changed state to up
.Jun 19 06:03:41.274: %OSPF-5-ADJCHG: Process 1, Nbr 192.168.1.1 on Serial0/0/0 from LOADING to FULL, Loading Done
```

d. Verify that interface S0/0/0 on both Branch1 and Central routers is up/up and is configured with PPP encapsulation.

What is the status of the PPP Link Control Protocol (LCP)? ____________________

Which Network Control Protocol (NCP) protocols have been negotiated?

_______________________________________________

```
Branch1# show interfaces s0/0/0
Serial0/0/0 is up, line protocol is up
  Hardware is WIC MBRD Serial
  Internet address is 10.1.1.1/30
  MTU 1500 bytes, BW 1544 Kbit/sec, DLY 20000 usec,
     reliability 255/255, txload 1/255, rxload 1/255
  Encapsulation PPP, LCP Open
  Open: IPCP, CDPCP, loopback not set
  Keepalive set (10 sec)
  Last input 00:00:00, output 00:00:00, output hang never
  Last clearing of "show interface" counters 00:03:58
  Input queue: 0/75/0/0 (size/max/drops/flushes); Total output drops: 0
  Queueing strategy: fifo
  Output queue: 0/40 (size/max)
  5 minute input rate 0 bits/sec, 0 packets/sec
  5 minute output rate 0 bits/sec, 0 packets/sec
     77 packets input, 4636 bytes, 0 no buffer
     Received 0 broadcasts (0 IP multicasts)
     0 runts, 0 giants, 0 throttles
     0 input errors, 0 CRC, 0 frame, 0 overrun, 0 ignored, 0 abort
     117 packets output, 5800 bytes, 0 underruns
     0 output errors, 0 collisions, 8 interface resets
     22 unknown protocol drops
     0 output buffer failures, 0 output buffers swapped out
     18 carrier transitions
     DCD=up  DSR=up  DTR=up  RTS=up  CTS=up

Central# show interfaces s0/0/0
Serial0/0/0 is up, line protocol is up
  Hardware is WIC MBRD Serial
  Internet address is 10.1.1.2/30
  MTU 1500 bytes, BW 1544 Kbit/sec, DLY 20000 usec,
     reliability 255/255, txload 1/255, rxload 1/255
```

```
Encapsulation PPP, LCP Open
Open: IPCP, CDPCP, loopback not set
Keepalive set (10 sec)
Last input 00:00:02, output 00:00:03, output hang never
Last clearing of "show interface" counters 00:01:20
Input queue: 0/75/0/0 (size/max/drops/flushes); Total output drops: 0
Queueing strategy: fifo
Output queue: 0/40 (size/max)
5 minute input rate 0 bits/sec, 0 packets/sec
5 minute output rate 0 bits/sec, 0 packets/sec
   41 packets input, 2811 bytes, 0 no buffer
   Received 0 broadcasts (0 IP multicasts)
   0 runts, 0 giants, 0 throttles
   0 input errors, 0 CRC, 0 frame, 0 overrun, 0 ignored, 0 abort
   40 packets output, 2739 bytes, 0 underruns
   0 output errors, 0 collisions, 0 interface resets
   0 unknown protocol drops
   0 output buffer failures, 0 output buffers swapped out
   0 carrier transitions
   DCD=up  DSR=up  DTR=up  RTS=up  CTS=up
```

### Step 3: Intentionally break the serial connection.

a. Issue the **debug ppp** commands to observe the effects of changing the PPP configuration on the Branch1 router and the Central router.

```
Branch1# debug ppp negotiation
PPP protocol negotiation debugging is on
Branch1# debug ppp packet
PPP packet display debugging is on

Central# debug ppp negotiation
PPP protocol negotiation debugging is on
Central# debug ppp packet
PPP packet display debugging is on
```

b. Observe the debug PPP messages when traffic is flowing on the serial link between the Branch1 and Central routers.

```
Branch1#
Jun 20 02:20:45.795: Se0/0/0 PPP: O pkt type 0x0021, datagramsize 84
Jun 20 02:20:49.639: Se0/0/0 PPP: I pkt type 0x0021, datagramsize 84 link[ip]
Jun 20 02:20:50.147: Se0/0/0 LCP-FS: I ECHOREQ [Open] id 45 len 12 magic 0x73885AF2
Jun 20 02:20:50.147: Se0/0/0 LCP-FS: O ECHOREP [Open] id 45 len 12 magic 0x8CE1F65F
Jun 20 02:20:50.159: Se0/0/0 LCP: O ECHOREQ [Open] id 45 len 12 magic 0x8CE1F65F
Jun 20 02:20:50.159: Se0/0/0 LCP-FS: I ECHOREP [Open] id 45 len 12 magic 0x73885AF2
Jun 20 02:20:50.159: Se0/0/0 LCP-FS: Received id 45, sent id 45, line up

Central#
Jun 20 02:20:49.636: Se0/0/0 PPP: O pkt type 0x0021, datagramsize 84
Jun 20 02:20:50.148: Se0/0/0 LCP: O ECHOREQ [Open] id 45 len 12 magic 0x73885AF2
Jun 20 02:20:50.148: Se0/0/0 LCP-FS: I ECHOREP [Open] id 45 len 12 magic 0x8CE1F65F
Jun 20 02:20:50.148: Se0/0/0 LCP-FS: Received id 45, sent id 45, line up
```

```
Jun 20 02:20:50.160: Se0/0/0 LCP-FS: I ECHOREQ [Open] id 45 len 12 magic 0x8CE1F65F
Jun 20 02:20:50.160: Se0/0/0 LCP-FS: O ECHOREP [Open] id 45 len 12 magic 0x73885AF2
Jun 20 02:20:55.552: Se0/0/0 PPP: I pkt type 0x0021, datagramsize 84 link[ip]
```

c. Break the serial connection by returning the serial encapsulation to HDLC for interface S0/0/0 on the Branch1 router. Record the command used to change the encapsulation to HDLC.

_______________________________________________

d. Observe the debug PPP messages on the Branch1 router. The serial connection has terminated, and the line protocol is down. The route to 10.1.1.2 (Central) has been removed from the routing table.

```
Jun 20 02:29:50.295: Se0/0/0 PPP DISC: Lower Layer disconnected
Jun 20 02:29:50.295: PPP: NET STOP send to AAA.
Jun 20 02:29:50.299: Se0/0/0 IPCP: Event[DOWN] State[Open to Starting]
Jun 20 02:29:50.299: Se0/0/0 IPCP: Event[CLOSE] State[Starting to Initial]
Jun 20 02:29:50.299: Se0/0/0 CDPCP: Event[DOWN] State[Open to Starting]
Jun 20 02:29:50.299: Se0/0/0 CDPCP: Event[CLOSE] State[Starting to Initial]
Jun 20 02:29:50.29
Branch1(config-if)#9: Se0/0/0 LCP: O TERMREQ [Open] id 7 len 4
Jun 20 02:29:50.299: Se0/0/0 LCP: Event[CLOSE] State[Open to Closing]
Jun 20 02:29:50.299: Se0/0/0 PPP: Phase is TERMINATING
Jun 20 02:29:50.299: Se0/0/0 Deleted neighbor route from AVL tree: topoid 0, address
10.1.1.2
Jun 20 02:29:50.299: Se0/0/0 IPCP: Remove route to 10.1.1.2
Jun 20 02:29:50.299: Se0/0/0 LCP: Event[DOWN] State[Closing to Initial]
Jun 20 02:29:50.299: Se0/0/0 PPP: Phase is DOWN
Branch1(config-if)#
Jun 20 02:30:17.083: %LINEPROTO-5-UPDOWN: Line protocol on Interface Serial0/0/0,
changed state to down
Jun 20 02:30:17.083: %OSPF-5-ADJCHG: Process 1, Nbr 209.165.200.225 on Serial0/0/0
from FULL to DOWN, Neighbor Down: Interface down or detached
```

e. Observe the debug PPP messages on the Central router. The Central router continues to attempt to establish a connection with Branch1 as indicated by the debug messages. When the interfaces are unable to establish a connection, the interfaces go back down again. Furthermore, OSPF cannot establish an adjacency with its neighbor due to the mismatched serial encapsulation.

```
Jun 20 02:29:50.296: Se0/0/0 PPP: Sending cstate DOWN notification
Jun 20 02:29:50.296: Se0/0/0 PPP: Processing CstateDown message
Jun 20 02:29:50.296: Se0/0/0 PPP DISC: Lower Layer disconnected
Jun 20 02:29:50.296: PPP: NET STOP send to AAA.
Jun 20 02:29:50.296: Se0/0/0 IPCP: Event[DOWN] State[Open to Starting]
Jun 20 02:29:50.296: Se0/0/0 IPCP: Event[CLOSE] State[Starting to Initial]
Jun 20 02:29:50.296: Se0/0/0 CDPCP: Event[DOWN] State[Open to Starting]
Jun 20 02:29:50.296: Se0/0/0 CDPCP: Event[CLOSE] State[Starting to Initial]
Jun 20 02:29:50.296: Se0/0/0 LCP: O TERMREQ [Open] id 2 len 4
Jun 20 02:29:50.296: Se0/0/0 LCP: Event[CLOSE] State[Open to Closing]
Jun 20 02:29:50.296: Se0/0/0 PPP: Phase is TERMINATING
Jun 20 02:29:50.296: Se0/0/0 Deleted neighbor route from AVL tree: topoid 0, address
10.1.1.1
Jun 20 02:29:50.296: Se0/0/0 IPCP: Remove route to 10.1.1.1
Jun 20 02:29:50.296: %OSPF-5-ADJCHG: Process 1, Nbr 192.168.1.1 on Serial0/0/0 from
FULL to DOWN, Neighbor Down: Interface down or detached
Jun 20 02:29:50.296: Se0/0/0 LCP: Event[DOWN] State[Closing to Initial]
Jun 20 02:29:50.296: Se0/0/0 PPP: Phase is DOWN
```

```
Jun 20 02:29:52.296: %LINEPROTO-5-UPDOWN: Line protocol on Interface Serial0/0/0,
changed state to down
.Jun 20 02:29:52.296: Se0/0/0 PPP: Sending cstate UP notification
.Jun 20 02:29:52.296: Se0/0/0 PPP: Processing CstateUp message
.Jun 20 02:29:52.296: PPP: Alloc Context [29F9F32C]
.Jun 20 02:29:52.296: ppp3 PPP: Phase is ESTABLISHING
.Jun 20 02:29:52.296: Se0/0/0 PPP: Using default call direction
.Jun 20 02:29:52.296: Se0/0/0 PPP: Treating connection as a dedicated line
.Jun 20 02:29:52.296: Se0/0/0 PPP: Session handle[60000003] Session id[3]
.Jun 20 02:29:52.296: Se0/0/0 LCP: Event[OPEN] State[Initial to Starting]
.Jun 20 02:29:52.296: Se0/0/0 LCP: O CONFREQ [Starting] id 1 len 10
.Jun 20 02:29:52.296: Se0/0/0 LCP:    MagicNumber 0x7397843B (0x05067397843B)
.Jun 20 02:29:52.296: Se0/0/0 LCP:Event[UP] State[Starting to REQsent]
.Jun 20 02:29:54.308: Se0/0/0 LCP: O CONFREQ [REQsent] id 2 len 10
.Jun 20 02:29:54.308: Se0/0/0 LCP:    MagicNumber 0x7397843B (0x05067397843B)
.Jun 20 02:29:54.308: Se0/0/0 LCP: Event[Timeout+] State[REQsent to REQsent]
.Jun 20 02:29:56.080: Se0/0/0 PPP: I pkt type 0x008F, datagramsize 24 link[illegal]
.Jun 20 02:29:56.080: Se0/0/0 UNKNOWN(0x008F): Non-NCP packet, discarding
<output omitted>
.Jun 20 02:30:10.436: Se0/0/0 LCP: O CONFREQ [REQsent] id 10 len 10
.Jun 20 02:30:10.436: Se0/0/0 LCP:    MagicNumber 0x7397843B (0x05067397843B)
.Jun 20 02:30:10.436: Se0/0/0 LCP: Event[Timeout+] State[REQsent to REQsent]
.Jun 20 02:30:12.452: Se0/0/0 PPP DISC: LCP failed to negotiate
.Jun 20 02:30:12.452: PPP: NET STOP send to AAA.
.Jun 20 02:30:12.452: Se0/0/0 LCP: Event[Timeout-] State[REQsent to Stopped]
.Jun 20 02:30:12.452: Se0/0/0 LCP: Event[DOWN] State[Stopped to Starting]
.Jun 20 02:30:12.452: Se0/0/0 PPP: Phase is DOWN
.Jun 20 02:30:14.452: PPP: Alloc Context [29F9F32C]
.Jun 20 02:30:14.452: ppp4 PPP: Phase is ESTABLISHING
.Jun 20 02:30:14.452: Se0/0/0 PPP: Using default call direction
.Jun 20 02:30:14.452: Se0/0/0 PPP: Treating connection as a dedicated line
.Jun 20 02:30:14.452: Se0/0/0 PPP: Session handle[6E000004] Session id[4]
.Jun 20 02:30:14.452: Se0/0/0 LCP: Event[OPEN] State[Initial to Starting]
.Jun 20 02:30:14.452: Se0/0/0 LCP: O CONFREQ [Starting] id 1 len 10
.Jun 20 02:30:14.452: Se0/0/0 LCP:    MagicNumber 0x7397DADA (0x05067397DADA)
.Jun 20 02:30:14.452: Se0/0/0 LCP: Event[UP] State[Starting to REQsent]
.Jun 20 02:30:16.080: Se0/0/0 PPP: I pkt type 0x008F, datagramsize 24 link[illegal]
.Jun 20 02:30:16.080: Se0/0/0 UNKNOWN(0x008F): Non-NCP packet, discarding
<output omitted>
.Jun 20 02:30:32.580: Se0/0/0 LCP: O CONFREQ [REQsent] id 10 len 10
.Jun 20 02:30:32.580: Se0/0/0 LCP:    MagicNumber 0x7397DADA (0x05067397DADA)
.Jun 20 02:30:32.580: Se0/0/0 LCP: Event[Timeout+] State[REQsent to REQsent]
.Jun 20 02:30:34.596: Se0/0/0 PPP DISC: LCP failed to negotiate
.Jun 20 02:30:34.596: PPP: NET STOP send to AAA.
.Jun 20 02:30:34.596: Se0/0/0 LCP: Event[Timeout-] State[REQsent to Stopped]
.Jun 20 02:30:34.596: Se0/0/0 LCP: Event[DOWN] State[Stopped to Starting]
.Jun 20 02:30:34.596: Se0/0/0 PPP: Phase is DOWN
.Jun 20 02:30:36.080: Se0/0/0 PPP: I pkt type 0x008F, discarded, PPP not running
.Jun 20 02:30:36.596: PPP: Alloc Context [29F9F32C]
.Jun 20 02:30:36.596: ppp5 PPP: Phase is ESTABLISHING
.Jun 20 02:30:36.596: Se0/0/0 PPP: Using default call direction
```

```
.Jun 20 02:30:36.596: Se0/0/0 PPP: Treating connection as a dedicated line
.Jun 20 02:30:36.596: Se0/0/0 PPP: Session handle[34000005] Session id[5]
.Jun 20 02:30:36.596: Se0/0/0 LCP: Event[OPEN] State[Initial to Starting]
```

What happens when one end of the serial link is encapsulated with PPP and the other end of the link is encapsulated with HDLC?

_______________________________________________

_______________________________________________

_______________________________________________

f. Issue the **encapsulation ppp** command on the S0/0/0 interface for the Branch1 router to correct mismatched encapsulation.

```
Branch1(config)# interface s0/0/0
Branch1(config-if)# encapsulation ppp
```

g. Observe the debug PPP messages from the Branch1 router as the Branch1 and Central routers establish a connection.

```
Branch1(config-if)#
Jun 20 03:01:57.399: %OSPF-5-ADJCHG: Process 1, Nbr 209.165.200.225 on Serial0/0/0
from FULL to DOWN, Neighbor Down: Interface down or detached
Jun 20 03:01:59.399: %LINEPROTO-5-UPDOWN: Line protocol on Interface Serial0/0/0,
changed state to down
Jun 20 03:01:59.399: Se0/0/0 PPP: Sending cstate UP notification
Jun 20 03:01:59.399: Se0/0/0 PPP: Processing CstateUp message
Jun 20 03:01:59.399: PPP: Alloc Context [30F8D4F0]
Jun 20 03:01:59.399: ppp9 PPP: Phase is ESTABLISHING
Jun 20 03:01:59.399: Se0/0/0 PPP: Using default call direction
Jun 20 03:01:59.399: Se0/0/0 PPP: Treating connection as a dedicated line
Jun 20 03:01:59.399: Se0/0/0 PPP: Session handle[BA000009] Session id[9]
Jun 20 03:01:59.399: Se0/0/0 LCP: Event[OPEN] State[Initial to Starting]
Jun 20 03:01:59.399: Se0/0/0 LCP: O CONFREQ [Starting] id 1 len 10
Jun 20 03:01:59.399: Se0/0/0 LCP:    MagicNumber 0x8D0EAC44 (0x05068D0EAC44)
Jun 20 03:01:59.399: Se0/0/0 LCP: Event[UP] State[Starting to REQsent]
Jun 20 03:01:59.407: Se0/0/0 PPP: I pkt type 0xC021, datagramsize 14 link[ppp]
Jun 20 03:01:59.407: Se0/0/0 LCP: I CONFREQ [REQsent] id 1 len 10
Jun 20 03:01:59.407: Se0/0/0 LCP:    MagicNumber 0x73B4F1AF (0x050673B4F1AF)
Jun 20 03:01:59.407: Se0/0/0 LCP: O CONFACK [REQsent] id 1 len 10
Jun 20 03:01:59.407: Se0/0/0 LCP:    MagicNumber 0x73B4F1AF (0x050673B4F1AF)
Jun 20 03:01:59.407: Se0/0/0 LCP: Event[Receive ConfReq+] State[REQsent to ACKsent]
Jun 20 03:01:59.407: Se0/0/0 PPP: I pkt type 0xC021, datagramsize 14 link[ppp]
Jun 20 03:01:59.407: Se0/0/0 LCP: I CONFACK [ACKsent] id 1 len 10
Jun 20 03:01:59.407: Se0/0/0 LCP:    MagicNumber 0x8D0EAC44 (0x05068D0EAC44)
Jun 20 03:01:59.407: Se0/0/0 LCP: Event[Receive ConfAck] State[ACKsent to Open]
Jun 20 03:01:59.439: Se0/0/0 PPP: Phase is FORWARDING, Attempting Forward
Jun 20 03:01:59.439: Se0/0/0 LCP: State is Open
Jun 20 03:01:59.439: Se0/0/0 PPP: Phase is ESTABLISHING, Finish LCP
Jun 20 03:01:59.439: %LINEPROTO-5-UPDOWN: Line protocol on Interface Serial0/0/0,
changed state to up
Jun 20 03:01:59.439: Se0/0/0 PPP: Outbound cdp packet dropped, line protocol not up
Jun 20 03:01:59.439: Se0/0/0 PPP: Phase is UP
```

```
Jun 20 03:01:59.439: Se0/0/0 IPCP: Protocol configured, start CP. state[Initial]
Jun 20 03:01:59.439: Se0/0/0 IPCP: Event[OPEN] State[Initial to Starting]
Jun 20 03:01:59.439: Se0/0/0 IPCP: O CONFREQ [Starting] id 1 len 10
Jun 20 03:01:59.439: Se0/0/0 IPCP:    Address 10.1.1.1 (0x03060A010101)
Jun 20 03:01:59.439: Se0/0/0 IPCP: Event[UP] State[Starting to REQsent]
Jun 20 03:01:59.439: Se0/0/0 CDPCP: Protocol configured, start CP. state[Initial]
<output omitted>
Jun 20 03:01:59.471: Se0/0/0 Added to neighbor route AVL tree: topoid 0, address
10.1.1.2
Jun 20 03:01:59.471: Se0/0/0 IPCP: Install route to 10.1.1.2
Jun 20 03:01:59.471: Se0/0/0 PPP: O pkt type 0x0021, datagramsize 80
Jun 20 03:01:59.479: Se0/0/0 PPP: I pkt type 0x0021, datagramsize 80 link[ip]
Jun 20 03:01:59.479: Se0/0/0 PPP: O pkt type 0x0021, datagramsize 84
Jun 20 03:01:59.483: Se0/0/0 PPP: I pkt type 0x0021, datagramsize 84 link[ip]
Jun 20 03:01:59.483: Se0/0/0 PPP: O pkt type 0x0021, datagramsize 68
Jun 20 03:01:59.491: Se0/0/0 PPP: I pkt type 0x0021, datagramsize 68 link[ip]
Jun 20 03:01:59.491: Se0/0/0 PPP: O pkt type 0x0021, datagramsize 148
Jun 20 03:01:59.511: Se0/0/0 PPP: I pkt type 0x0021, datagramsize 148 link[ip]
Jun 20 03:01:59.511: %OSPF-5-ADJCHG:Process 1, Nbr 209.165.200.225 on Serial0/0/0 from
LOADING to FULL, Loading Done
Jun 20 03:01:59.511: Se0/0/0 PPP: O pkt type 0x0021, datagramsize 68
Jun 20 03:01:59.519: Se0/0/0 PPP: I pkt type 0x0021, datagramsize 60 link[ip]
```

h. Observe the debug PPP messages from the Central router as the Branch1 and Central routers establish a connection.

```
Jun 20 03:01:59.393: Se0/0/0 PPP: I pkt type 0xC021, datagramsize 14 link[ppp]
Jun 20 03:01:59.393: Se0/0/0 LCP: I CONFREQ [Open] id 1 len 10
Jun 20 03:01:59.393: Se0/0/0 LCP:    MagicNumber 0x8D0EAC44 (0x05068D0EAC44)
Jun 20 03:01:59.393: Se0/0/0 PPP DISC: PPP Renegotiating
Jun 20 03:01:59.393: PPP: NET STOP send to AAA.
Jun 20 03:01:59.393: Se0/0/0 LCP: Event[LCP Reneg] State[Open to Open]
Jun 20 03:01:59.393: Se0/0/0 IPCP: Event[DOWN] State[Open to Starting]
Jun 20 03:01:59.393: Se0/0/0 IPCP: Event[CLOSE] State[Starting to Initial]
Jun 20 03:01:59.393: Se0/0/0 CDPCP: Event[DOWN] State[Open to Starting]
Jun 20 03:01:59.393: Se0/0/0 CDPCP: Event[CLOSE] State[Starting to Initial]
Jun 20 03:01:59.393: Se0/0/0 LCP: Event[DOWN] State[Open to Starting]
Jun 20 03:01:59.393: %LINEPROTO-5-UPDOWN: Line protocol on Interface Serial0/0/0,
changed state to down
Jun 20 03:01:59.393: Se0/0/0 PPP: Outbound cdp packet dropped, NCP not negotiated
.Jun 20 03:01:59.393: Se0/0/0 PPP: Phase is DOWN
.Jun 20 03:01:59.393: Se0/0/0 Deleted neighbor route from AVL tree: topoid 0, address
10.1.1.1
.Jun 20 03:01:59.393: Se0/0/0 IPCP: Remove route to 10.1.1.1
.Jun 20 03:01:59.393: %OSPF-5-ADJCHG: Process 1, Nbr 192.168.1.1 on Serial0/0/0 from
FULL to DOWN, Neighbor Down: Interface down or detached
.Jun 20 03:01:59.397: PPP: Alloc Context [29F9F32C]
.Jun 20 03:01:59.397: ppp38 PPP: Phase is ESTABLISHING
.Jun 20 03:01:59.397: Se0/0/0 PPP: Using default call direction
.Jun 20 03:01:59.397: Se0/0/0 PPP: Treating connection as a dedicated line
<output omitted>
.Jun 20 03:01:59.401: Se0/0/0 LCP:    MagicNumber 0x73B4F1AF (0x050673B4F1AF)
.Jun 20 03:01:59.401: Se0/0/0 LCP: Event[Receive ConfAck] State[ACKsent to Open]
```

```
.Jun 20 03:01:59.433: Se0/0/0 PPP: Phase is FORWARDING, Attempting Forward
.Jun 20 03:01:59.433: Se0/0/0 LCP: State is Open
.Jun 20 03:01:59.433: Se0/0/0 PPP: I pkt type 0x8021, datagramsize 14 link[ip]
.Jun 20 03:01:59.433: Se0/0/0 PPP: Queue IPCP code[1] id[1]
.Jun 20 03:01:59.433: Se0/0/0 PPP: I pkt type 0x8207, datagramsize 8 link[cdp]
.Jun 20 03:01:59.433: Se0/0/0 PPP: Discarded CDPCP code[1] id[1]
.Jun 20 03:01:59.433: Se0/0/0 PPP: Phase is ESTABLISHING, Finish LCP
.Jun 20 03:01:59.433: %LINEPROTO-5-UPDOWN: Line protocol on Interface Serial0/0/0,
changed state to up
.Jun 20 03:01:59.433: Se0/0/0 PPP: Outbound cdp packet dropped, line protocol not up
.Jun 20 03:01:59.433: Se0/0/0 PPP: Phase is UP
.Jun 20 03:01:59.433: Se0/0/0 IPCP: Protocol configured, start CP. state[Initial]
.Jun 20 03:01:59.433: Se0/0/0 IPCP: Event[OPEN] State[Initial to Starting]
.Jun 20 03:01:59.433: Se0/0/0 IPCP: O CONFREQ [Starting] id 1 len 10
.Jun 20 03:01:59.433: Se0/0/0 IPCP:    Address 10.1.1.2 (0x03060A010102)
.Jun 20 03:01:59.433: Se0/0/0 IPCP: Event[UP] State[Starting to REQsent]
.Jun 20 03:01:59.433: Se0/0/0 CDPCP: Protocol configured, start CP. state[Initial]
.Jun 20 03:01:59.433: Se0/0/0 CDPCP: Event[OPEN] State[Initial to Starting]
.Jun 20 03:01:59.433: Se0/0/0 CDPCP: O CONFREQ [Starting] id 1 len 4
.Jun 20 03:01:59.433: Se0/0/0 CDPCP: Event[UP] State[Starting to REQsent]
<output omitted>
.Jun 20 03:01:59.465: Se0/0/0 IPCP: State is Open
.Jun 20 03:01:59.465: Se0/0/0 Added to neighbor route AVL tree: topoid 0, address
10.1.1.1
.Jun 20 03:01:59.465: Se0/0/0 IPCP: Install route to 10.1.1.1
.Jun 20 03:01:59.465: Se0/0/0 PPP: O pkt type 0x0021, datagramsize 80
.Jun 20 03:01:59.465: Se0/0/0 PPP: I pkt type 0x0021, datagramsize 80 link[ip]
.Jun 20 03:01:59.469: Se0/0/0 PPP: O pkt type 0x0021, datagramsize 84
.Jun 20 03:01:59.477: Se0/0/0 PPP: I pkt type 0x0021, datagramsize 84 link[ip]
.Jun 20 03:01:59.477: Se0/0/0 PPP: O pkt type 0x0021, datagramsize 68
.Jun 20 03:01:59.481: Se0/0/0 PPP: I pkt type 0x0021, datagramsize 68 link[ip]
.Jun 20 03:01:59.489: Se0/0/0 PPP: I pkt type 0x0021, datagramsize 148 link[ip]
.Jun 20 03:01:59.493: Se0/0/0 PPP: O pkt type 0x0021, datagramsize 148
.Jun 20 03:01:59.505: Se0/0/0 PPP: I pkt type 0x0021, datagramsize 68 link[ip]
.Jun 20 03:01:59.505: Se0/0/0 PPP: O pkt type 0x0021, datagramsize 60
.Jun 20 03:01:59.517: Se0/0/0 PPP: I pkt type 0x0021, datagramsize 88 link[ip]
.Jun 20 03:01:59.517: %OSPF-5-ADJCHG: Process 1, Nbr 192.168.1.1 on Serial0/0/0 from
LOADING to FULL, Loading Done
.Jun 20 03:01:59.561: Se0/0/0 PPP: O pkt type 0x0021, datagramsize 80
.Jun 20 03:01:59.569: Se0/0/0 PPP: I pkt type 0x0021, datagramsize 80 link[ip]
Jun 20 03:02:01.445: Se0/0/0 PPP: I pkt type 0x8207, datagramsize 8 link[cdp]
Jun 20 03:02:01.445: Se0/0/0 CDPCP: I CONFREQ [ACKrcvd] id 2 len 4
Jun 20 03:02:01.445: Se0/0/0 CDPCP: O CONFACK [ACKrcvd] id 2 len 4
Jun 20 03:02:01.445: Se0/0/0 CDPCP: Event[Receive ConfReq+] State[ACKrcvd to Open]
Jun 20 03:02:01.449: Se0/0/0 CDPCP: State is Open
Jun 20 03:02:01.561: Se0/0/0 PPP: O pkt type 0x0021, datagramsize 80
Jun 20 03:02:01.569: Se0/0/0 PPP: I pkt type 0x0021, datagramsize 80 link[ip]
Jun 20 03:02:02.017: Se0/0/0 PPP: O pkt type 0x0021, datagramsize 68
Jun 20 03:02:02.897: Se0/0/0 PPP: I pkt type 0x0021, datagramsize 112 link[ip]
Jun 20 03:02:03.561: Se0/0/0 PPP: O pkt type 0x0021, datagramsize 80
```

From the debug message, what phases does PPP go through when the other end of the serial link on the Central router is configured with PPP encapsulation?

____________________________________________________________

____________________________________________________________

What happens when PPP encapsulation is configured on each end of the serial link?

____________________________________________________________

i. Issue the **undebug all** (or **u all**) command on the Branch1 and Central routers to turn off all debugging on both routers.

j. Issue the **show ip interface brief** command on the Branch1 and Central routers after the network converges. What is the status for interface S0/0/0 on both routers?

____________________________________________________________

k. Verify that the interface S0/0/0 on both Branch1 and Central routers are configured for PPP encapsulation.

Record the command to verify the PPP encapsulation in the space provided below.

____________________________________________________________

____________________________________________________________

l. Change the serial encapsulation for the link between the Central and Branch3 routers to PPP encapsulation.

```
Central(config)# interface s0/0/1
Central(config-if)# encapsulation ppp
Central(config-if)#
Jun 20 03:17:15.933: %OSPF-5-ADJCHG: Process 1, Nbr 192.168.3.1 on Serial0/0/1 from
FULL to DOWN, Neighbor Down: Interface down or detached
Jun 20 03:17:17.933: %LINEPROTO-5-UPDOWN: Line protocol on Interface Serial0/0/1,
changed state to down
Jun 20 03:17:23.741: %LINEPROTO-5-UPDOWN: Line protocol on Interface Serial0/0/1,
changed state to up
Jun 20 03:17:23.825: %OSPF-5-ADJCHG: Process 1, Nbr 192.168.3.1 on Serial0/0/1 from
LOADING to FULL, Loading Done
```

```
Branch3(config)# interface s0/0/1
Branch3(config-if)# encapsulation ppp
Branch3(config-if)#
Jun 20 03:17:21.744: %OSPF-5-ADJCHG: Process 1, Nbr 209.165.200.225 on Serial0/0/1
from FULL to DOWN, Neighbor Down: Interface down or detached
Jun 20 03:17:21.948: %LINEPROTO-5-UPDOWN: Line protocol on Interface Serial0/0/1,
changed state to down
.Jun 20 03:17:21.964: %LINEPROTO-5-UPDOWN: Line protocol on Interface Serial0/0/1,
changed state to up
.Jun 20 03:17:23.812: %OSPF-5-ADJCHG: Process 1, Nbr 209.165.200.225 on Serial0/0/1
from LOADING to FULL, Loading Done
```

m. Verify that end-to-end connectivity is restored before continuing to Part 3.

## Part 3: Configure PPP CHAP Authentication

### Step 1: Verify that PPP encapsulation is configured on all serial interfaces.

Record the command used to verify that PPP encapsulation is configured.

_______________________________________________

### Step 2: Configure PPP CHAP authentication for the link between the Central router and the Branch3 router.

a. Configure a username for CHAP authentication.

```
Central(config)# username Branch3 password cisco
Branch3(config)# username Central password cisco
```

b. Issue the **debug ppp** commands on the Branch3 router to observe the process, which is associated with authentication.

```
Branch3# debug ppp negotiation
PPP protocol negotiation debugging is on
Branch3# debug ppp packet
PPP packet display debugging is on
```

c. Configure the interface S0/0/1 on Branch3 for CHAP authentication.

```
Branch3(config)# interface s0/0/1
Branch3(config-if)# ppp authentication chap
```

d. Examine the debug PPP messages on the Branch3 router during the negotiation with the Central router.

```
Branch3(config-if)#
Jun 20 04:25:02.079: Se0/0/1 PPP DISC: Authentication configuration changed
Jun 20 04:25:02.079: PPP: NET STOP send to AAA.
Jun 20 04:25:02.079: Se0/0/1 IPCP: Event[DOWN] State[Open to Starting]
Jun 20 04:25:02.079: Se0/0/1 IPCP: Event[CLOSE] State[Starting to Initial]
Jun 20 04:25:02.079: Se0/0/1 CDPCP: Event[DOWN] State[Open to Starting]
Jun 20 04:25:02.079: Se0/0/1 CDPCP: Event[CLOSE] State[Starting to Initial]
Jun 20 04:25:02.079: Se0/0/1 LCP: Event[DOWN] State[Open to Starting]
Jun 20 04:25:02.079: %LINEPROTO-5-UPDOWN: Line protocol on Interface Serial0/0/1,
changed state to down
Jun 20 04:25:02.079: Se0/0/1 PPP: Outbound cdp packet dropped, NCP not negotiated
.Jun 20 04:25:02.079: Se0/0/1 PPP: Phase is DOWN
.Jun 20 04:25:02.079: Se0/0/1 Deleted neighbor route from AVL tree: topoid 0, address
10.2.2.2
.Jun 20 04:25:02.079: Se0/0/1 IPCP: Remove route to 10.2.2.2
.Jun 20 04:25:02.079: %OSPF-5-ADJCHG: Process 1, Nbr 209.165.200.225 on Serial0/0/1
from FULL to DOWN, Neighbor Down: Interface down or detached
.Jun 20 04:25:02.083: PPP: Alloc Context [29F4DA8C]
.Jun 20 04:25:02.083: ppp73 PPP: Phase is ESTABLISHING
.Jun 20 04:25:02.083: Se0/0/1 PPP: Using default call direction
.Jun 20 04:25:02.083: Se0/0/1 PPP: Treating connection as a dedicated line
.Jun 20 04:25:02.083: Se0/0/1 PPP: Session handle[2700004D] Session id[73]
<output omitted>
.Jun 20 04:25:02.091: Se0/0/1 PPP: I pkt type 0xC021, datagramsize 19 link[ppp]
.Jun 20 04:25:02.091: Se0/0/1 LCP: I CONFACK [ACKsent] id 1 len 15
.Jun 20 04:25:02.091: Se0/0/1 LCP:    AuthProto CHAP (0x0305C22305)
.Jun 20 04:25:02.091: Se0/0/1 LCP:    MagicNumber 0xF7B20F10 (0x0506F7B20F10)
```

```
.Jun 20 04:25:02.091: Se0/0/1 LCP: Event[Receive ConfAck] State[ACKsent to Open]
.Jun 20 04:25:02.123: Se0/0/1 PPP: Phase is AUTHENTICATING, by this end
.Jun 20 04:25:02.123: Se0/0/1 CHAP: O CHALLENGE id 1 len 28 from "Branch3"
.Jun 20 04:25:02.123: Se0/0/1 LCP: State is Open
.Jun 20 04:25:02.127: Se0/0/1 PPP: I pkt type 0xC223, datagramsize 32 link[ppp]
.Jun 20 04:25:02.127: Se0/0/1 CHAP: I RESPONSE id 1 len 28 from "Central"
.Jun 20 04:25:02.127: Se0/0/1 PPP: Phase is FORWARDING, Attempting Forward
.Jun 20 04:25:02.127: Se0/0/1 PPP: Phase is AUTHENTICATING, Unauthenticated User
.Jun 20 04:25:02.127: Se0/0/1 PPP: Sent CHAP LOGIN Request
.Jun 20 04:25:02.127: Se0/0/1 PPP: Received LOGIN Response PASS
.Jun 20 04:25:02.127: Se0/0/1 IPCP: Authorizing CP
.Jun 20 04:25:02.127: Se0/0/1 IPCP: CP stalled on event[Authorize CP]
.Jun 20 04:25:02.127: Se0/0/1 IPCP: CP unstall
.Jun 20 04:25:02.127: Se0/0/1 PPP: Phase is FORWARDING, Attempting Forward
.Jun 20 04:25:02.135: Se0/0/1 PPP: Phase is AUTHENTICATING, Authenticated User
.Jun 20 04:25:02.135: Se0/0/1 CHAP: O SUCCESS id 1 len 4
.Jun 20 04:25:02.135: %LINEPROTO-5-UPDOWN: Line protocol on Interface Serial0/0/1,
changed state to up
.Jun 20 04:25:02.135: Se0/0/1 PPP: Outbound cdp packet dropped, line protocol not up
.Jun 20 04:25:02.135: Se0/0/1 PPP: Phase is UP
.Jun 20 04:25:02.135: Se0/0/1 IPCP: Protocol configured, start CP. state[Initial]
.Jun 20 04:25:02.135: Se0/0/1 IPCP: Event[OPEN] State[Initial to Starting]
.Jun 20 04:25:02.135: Se0/0/1 IPCP: O CONFREQ [Starting] id 1 len 10
<output omitted>
.Jun 20 04:25:02.143: Se0/0/1 CDPCP: I CONFACK [ACKsent] id 1 len 4
.Jun 20 04:25:02.143: Se0/0/1 CDPCP: Event[Receive ConfAck] State[ACKsent to Open]
.Jun 20 04:25:02.155: Se0/0/1 IPCP: State is Open
.Jun 20 04:25:02.155: Se0/0/1 CDPCP: State is Open
.Jun 20 04:25:02.155: Se0/0/1 Added to neighbor route AVL tree: topoid 0, address
10.2.2.2
.Jun 20 04:25:02.155: Se0/0/1 IPCP: Install route to 10.2.2.2
.Jun 20 04:25:02.155: Se0/0/1 PPP: O pkt type 0x0021, datagramsize 80
.Jun 20 04:25:02.155: Se0/0/1 PPP: I pkt type 0x0021, datagramsize 80 link[ip]
.Jun 20 04:25:02.155: Se0/0/1 PPP: O pkt type 0x0021, datagramsize 84
.Jun 20 04:25:02.167: Se0/0/1 PPP: I pkt type 0x0021, datagramsize 84 link[ip]
.Jun 20 04:25:02.167: Se0/0/1 PPP: O pkt type 0x0021, datagramsize 68
.Jun 20 04:25:02.171: Se0/0/1 PPP: I pkt type 0x0021, datagramsize 68 link[ip]
.Jun 20 04:25:02.171: Se0/0/1 PPP: O pkt type 0x0021, datagramsize 148
.Jun 20 04:25:02.191: Se0/0/1 PPP: I pkt type 0x0021, datagramsize 148 link[ip]
.Jun 20 04:25:02.191: %OSPF-5-ADJCHG: Process 1, Nbr 209.165.200.225 on Serial0/0/1
from LOADING to FULL, Loading Done
.Jun 20 04:25:02.191: Se0/0/1 PPP: O pkt type 0x0021, datagramsize 68
.Jun 20 04:25:02.571: Se0/0/1 PPP: O pkt type 0x0021, datagramsize 80
.Jun 20 04:25:03.155: Se0/0/1 PPP: I pkt type 0x0207, datagramsize 333 link[cdp]
.Jun 20 04:25:03.155: Se0/0/1 PPP: O pkt type 0x0207, datagramsize 339
.Jun 20 04:25:04.155: Se0/0/1 PPP: O pkt type 0x0207, datagramsize 339
```

From the PPP debug messages, what phases did the Branch3 router go through before the link is up with the Central router?

____________________________________________________________________________

____________________________________________________________________________

e. Issue the **debug ppp authentication** command to observe the CHAP authentication messages on the Central router.

```
Central# debug ppp authentication
PPP authentication debugging is on
```

f. Configure CHAP authentication on S0/0/1 on the Central router.

g. Observe the debug PPP messages relating to CHAP authentication on the Central router.

```
Central(config-if)#
.Jun 20 05:05:16.057: %LINEPROTO-5-UPDOWN: Line protocol on Interface Serial0/0/1,
changed state to down
.Jun 20 05:05:16.061: %OSPF-5-ADJCHG: Process 1, Nbr 192.168.3.1 on Serial0/0/1 from
FULL to DOWN, Neighbor Down: Interface down or detached
.Jun 20 05:05:16.061: Se0/0/1 PPP: Using default call direction
.Jun 20 05:05:16.061: Se0/0/1 PPP: Treating connection as a dedicated line
.Jun 20 05:05:16.061: Se0/0/1 PPP: Session handle[12000078] Session id[112]
.Jun 20 05:05:16.081: Se0/0/1 CHAP: O CHALLENGE id 1 len 28 from "Central"
.Jun 20 05:05:16.089: Se0/0/1 CHAP: I CHALLENGE id 1 len 28 from "Branch3"
.Jun 20 05:05:16.089: Se0/0/1 PPP: Sent CHAP SENDAUTH Request
.Jun 20 05:05:16.089: Se0/0/1 PPP: Received SENDAUTH Response PASS
.Jun 20 05:05:16.089: Se0/0/1 CHAP: Using hostname from configured hostname
.Jun 20 05:05:16.089: Se0/0/1 CHAP: Using password from AAA
.Jun 20 05:05:16.089: Se0/0/1 CHAP: O RESPONSE id 1 len 28 from "Central"
.Jun 20 05:05:16.093: Se0/0/1 CHAP: I RESPONSE id 1 len 28 from "Branch3"
.Jun 20 05:05:16.093: Se0/0/1 PPP: Sent CHAP LOGIN Request
.Jun 20 05:05:16.093: Se0/0/1 PPP: Received LOGIN Response PASS
.Jun 20 05:05:16.093: Se0/0/1 CHAP: O SUCCESS id 1 len 4
.Jun 20 05:05:16.097: Se0/0/1 CHAP: I SUCCESS id 1 len 4
.Jun 20 05:05:16.097: %LINEPROTO-5-UPDOWN: Line protocol on Interface Serial0/0/1,
changed state to up
.Jun 20 05:05:16.165: %OSPF-5-ADJCHG: Process 1, Nbr 192.168.3.1 on Serial0/0/1 from
LOADING to FULL, Loading Done
```

h. Issue the **undebug all** (or **u all**) command on the Central and Branch3 routers to turn off all debugging.

```
Central# undebug all
All possible debugging has been turned off
```

## Step 3: Intentionally break the serial link configured with authentication.

a. On the Central router, configure a username for use with Branch1. Assign **cisco** as the password.

```
Central(config)# username Branch1 password cisco
```

b. On the Central and Branch1 routers, configure CHAP authentication on interface S0/0/0. What is happening with the interface?

____________________________________________________________

**Note**: To speed up the process, shut down the interface and enable it again.

c. Use a **debug ppp negotiation** command to examine what is happening.

```
Central# debug ppp negotiation
PPP protocol negotiation debugging is on
Central(config-if)#
.Jun 20 05:25:26.229: Se0/0/0 PPP: Missed a Link-Up transition, starting PPP
.Jun 20 05:25:26.229: Se0/0/0 PPP: Processing FastStart message
.Jun 20 05:25:26.229: PPP: Alloc Context [29F9F32C]
```

```
.Jun 20 05:25:26.229: ppp145 PPP: Phase is ESTABLISHING
.Jun 20 05:25:26.229: Se0/0/0 PPP: Using default call direction
.Jun 20 05:25:26.229: Se0/0/0 PPP: Treating connection as a dedicated line
.Jun 20 05:25:26.229: Se0/0/0 PPP: Session handle[6000009C] Session id[145]
.Jun 20 05:25:26.229: Se0/0/0 LCP: Event[OPEN] State[Initial to Starting]
.Jun 20 05:25:26.229: Se0/0/0 LCP: O CONFREQ [Starting] id 1 len 15
.Jun 20 05:25:26.229: Se0/0/0 LCP:    AuthProto CHAP (0x0305C22305)
.Jun 20 05:25:26.229: Se0/0/0 LCP:    MagicNumber 0x74385C31 (0x050674385C31)
.Jun 20 05:25:26.229: Se0/0/0 LCP: Event[UP] State[Starting to REQsent]
.Jun 20 05:25:26.229: Se0/0/0 LCP: I CONFREQ [REQsent] id 1 len 10
.Jun 20 05:25:26.229: Se0/0/0 LCP:    MagicNumber 0x8D920101 (0x05068D920101)
.Jun 20 05:25:26.229: Se0/0/0 LCP: O CONFACK [REQsent] id 1 len 10
.Jun 20 05:25:26.229: Se0/0/0 LCP:    MagicNumber 0x8D920101 (0x05068D920101)
.Jun 20 05:25:26.229: Se0/0/0 LCP: Event[Receive ConfReq+] State[REQsent to ACKsent]
.Jun 20 05:25:26.233: Se0/0/0 LCP: I CONFACK [ACKsent] id 1 len 15
.Jun 20 05:25:26.233: Se0/0/0 LCP:    AuthProto CHAP (0x0305C22305)
.Jun 20 05:25:26.233: Se0/0/0 LCP:    MagicNumber 0x74385C31 (0x050674385C31)
.Jun 20 05:25:26.233: Se0/0/0 LCP: Event[Receive ConfAck] State[ACKsent to Open]
.Jun 20 05:25:26.261: Se0/0/0 PPP: Phase is AUTHENTICATING, by this end
.Jun 20 05:25:26.261: Se0/0/0 CHAP: O CHALLENGE id 1 len 28 from "Central"
.Jun 20 05:25:26.261: Se0/0/0 LCP: State is Open
.Jun 20 05:25:26.265: Se0/0/0 LCP: I TERMREQ [Open] id 2 len 4
.Jun 20 05:25:26.265: Se0/0/0 PPP DISC: Received LCP TERMREQ from peer
.Jun 20 05:25:26.265: PPP: NET STOP send to AAA.
.Jun 20 05:25:26.265: Se0/0/0 PPP: Phase is TERMINATING
.Jun 20 05:25:26.265: Se0/0/0 LCP: O TERMACK [Open] id 2 len 4
.Jun 20 05:25:26.265: Se0/0/0 LCP: Event[Receive TermReq] State[Open to Stopping]
.Jun 20 05:25:26.265: Se0/0/0 PPP: Sending cstate DOWN notification
.Jun 20 05:25:26.265: Se0/0/0 PPP: Processing CstateDown message
.Jun 20 05:25:26.265: Se0/0/0 LCP: Event[CLOSE] State[Stopping to Closing]
.Jun 20 05:25:26.265: Se0/0/0 LCP: Event[DOWN] State[Closing to Initial]
.Jun 20 05:25:26.265: Se0/0/0 PPP: Phase is DOWN
```

Explain what is causing the link to terminate. Correct the issue and document the command issued to correct the issue in the space provided below.

______________________________________________________________________

______________________________________________________________________

______________________________________________________________________

d. Issue the **undebug all** command on all routers to turn off debugging.

e. Verify end-to-end connectivity.

## Reflection

1. What are the indicators that you may have a serial encapsulation mismatch on a serial link?

_______________________________________________

2. What are the indicators that you may have an authentication mismatch on a serial link?

_______________________________________________

## Router Interface Summary Table

| Router Interface Summary | | | | |
|---|---|---|---|---|
| **Router Model** | **Ethernet Interface #1** | **Ethernet Interface #2** | **Serial Interface #1** | **Serial Interface #2** |
| 1800 | Fast Ethernet 0/0 (F0/0) | Fast Ethernet 0/1 (F0/1) | Serial 0/0/0 (S0/0/0) | Serial 0/0/1 (S0/0/1) |
| 1900 | Gigabit Ethernet 0/0 (G0/0) | Gigabit Ethernet 0/1 (G0/1) | Serial 0/0/0 (S0/0/0) | Serial 0/0/1 (S0/0/1) |
| 2801 | Fast Ethernet 0/0 (F0/0) | Fast Ethernet 0/1 (F0/1) | Serial 0/1/0 (S0/1/0) | Serial 0/1/1 (S0/1/1) |
| 2811 | Fast Ethernet 0/0 (F0/0) | Fast Ethernet 0/1 (F0/1) | Serial 0/0/0 (S0/0/0) | Serial 0/0/1 (S0/0/1) |
| 2900 | Gigabit Ethernet 0/0 (G0/0) | Gigabit Ethernet 0/1 (G0/1) | Serial 0/0/0 (S0/0/0) | Serial 0/0/1 (S0/0/1) |
| **Note**: To find out how the router is configured, look at the interfaces to identify the type of router and how many interfaces the router has. There is no way to effectively list all the combinations of configurations for each router class. This table includes identifiers for the possible combinations of Ethernet and Serial interfaces in the device. The table does not include any other type of interface, even though a specific router may contain one. An example of this might be an ISDN BRI interface. The string in parenthesis is the legal abbreviation that can be used in Cisco IOS commands to represent the interface. | | | | |

# 3.4.1.5 Lab – Troubleshooting Basic PPP with Authentication

## Topology

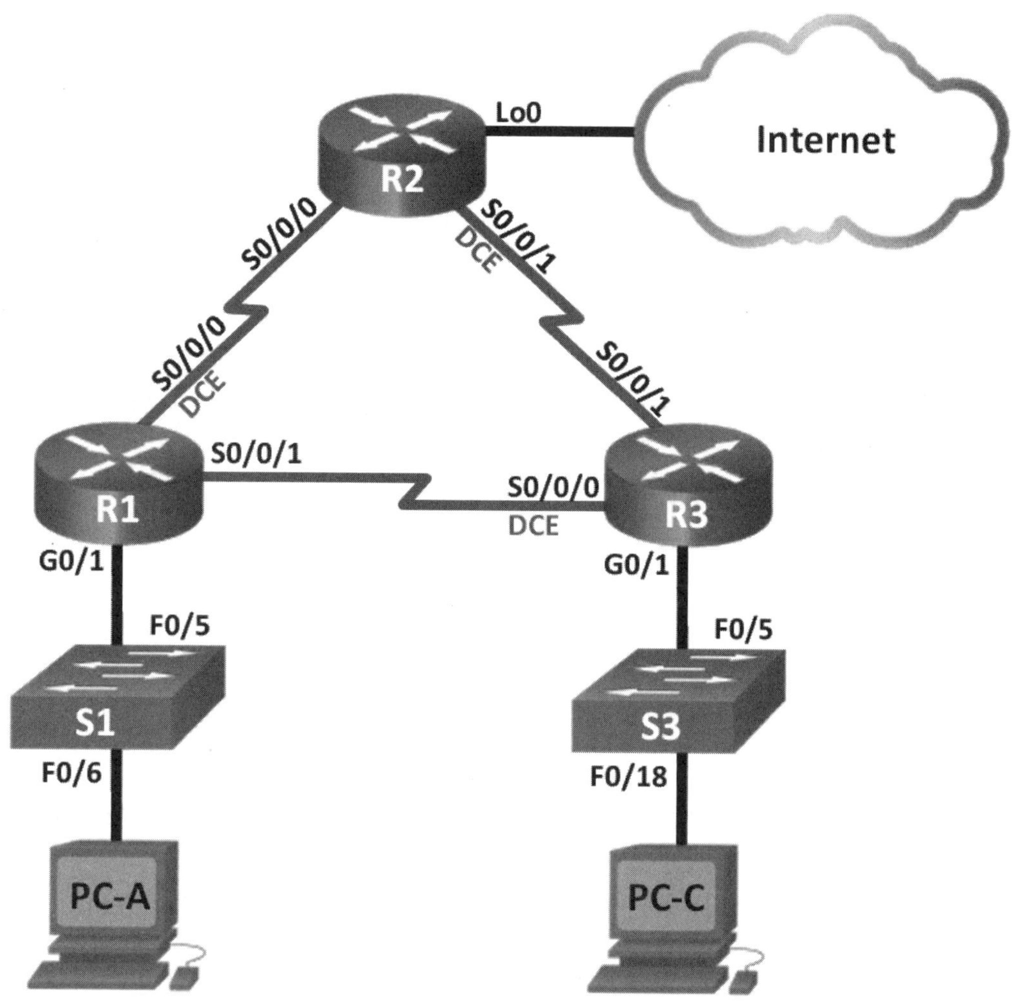


## Addressing Table

| Device | Interface | IP Address | Subnet Mask | Default Gateway |
|---|---|---|---|---|
| R1 | G0/1 | 192.168.1.1 | 255.255.255.0 | N/A |
| | S0/0/0 (DCE) | 192.168.12.1 | 255.255.255.252 | N/A |
| | S0/0/1 | 192.168.13.1 | 255.255.255.252 | N/A |
| R2 | Lo0 | 209.165.200.225 | 255.255.255.252 | N/A |
| | S0/0/0 | 192.168.12.2 | 255.255.255.252 | N/A |
| | S0/0/1 (DCE) | 192.168.23.1 | 255.255.255.252 | N/A |
| R3 | G0/1 | 192.168.3.1 | 255.255.255.0 | N/A |
| | S0/0/0 (DCE) | 192.168.13.2 | 255.255.255.252 | N/A |
| | S0/0/1 | 192.168.23.2 | 255.255.255.252 | N/A |
| PC-A | NIC | 192.168.1.3 | 255.255.255.0 | 192.168.1.1 |
| PC-C | NIC | 192.168.3.3 | 255.255.255.0 | 192.168.3.1 |

## Objectives

**Part 1: Build the Network and Load Device Configurations**

**Part 2: Troubleshoot the Data Link Layer**

**Part 3: Troubleshoot the Network Layer**

## Background / Scenario

The routers at your company were configured by an inexperienced network engineer. Several errors in the configuration have resulted in connectivity issues. Your manager has asked you to troubleshoot and correct the configuration errors and document your work. Using your knowledge of PPP and standard testing methods, find and correct the errors. Ensure that all of the serial links use PPP CHAP authentication, and that all of the networks are reachable.

**Note**: The routers used with CCNA hands-on labs are Cisco 1941 Integrated Services Routers (ISRs) with Cisco IOS Release 15.2(4)M3 (universalk9 image). The switches used are Cisco Catalyst 2960s with Cisco IOS Release 15.0(2) (lanbasek9 image). Other routers, switches, and Cisco IOS versions can be used. Depending on the model and Cisco IOS version, the commands available and output produced might vary from what is shown in the labs. Refer to the Router Interface Summary Table at the end of this lab for the correct interface identifiers.

**Note**: Make sure that the routers and switches have been erased and have no startup configurations. If you are unsure, contact your instructor.

## Required Resources

- 3 Routers (Cisco 1941 with Cisco IOS Release 15.2(4)M3 universal image or comparable)
- 2 Switches (Cisco 2960 with Cisco IOS Release 15.0(2) lanbasek9 image or comparable)
- 2 PCs (Windows 7, Vista, or XP with a terminal emulation program, such as Tera Term)
- Console cables to configure the Cisco IOS devices via the console ports
- Ethernet and serial cables as shown in the topology

# Part 1: Build the Network and Load Device Configurations

In Part 1, you will set up the network topology, configure basic settings on the PC hosts, and load configurations on the routers.

### Step 1: Cable the network as shown in the topology.

### Step 2: Configure the PC hosts.

### Step 3: Load router configurations.

Load the following configurations into the appropriate router. All routers have the same passwords. The privileged EXEC mode password is **class**. The password for console and vty access is **cisco**. All serial interfaces should be configured with PPP encapsulation and authenticated with CHAP using the password of **chap123**.

**Router R1 Configuration:**

```
hostname R1
enable secret class
no ip domain lookup
banner motd #Unauthorized Access is Prohibited!#
username R2 password chap123
username R3 password chap123
interface g0/1
 ip address 192.168.1.1 255.255.255.0
 no shutdown
interface s0/0/0
 ip address 192.168.12.1 255.255.255.252
 clock rate 128000
 encapsulation ppp
 ppp authentication chap

interface s0/0/1
 ip address 192.168.31.1 255.255.255.252

 encapsulation ppp
 ppp authentication pap


exit
router ospf 1
 router-id 1.1.1.1
 network 192.168.1.0 0.0.0.255 area 0
 network 192.168.12.0 0.0.0.3 area 0
 network 192.168.13.0 0.0.0.3 area 0
 passive-interface g0/1
 exit
line con 0
 password cisco
 logging synchronous
 login
line vty 0 4
 password cisco
 login
```

**Router R2 Configuration:**

```
hostname R2
enable secret class
no ip domain lookup
banner motd #Unauthorized Access is Prohibited!#
username R1 password chap123
username r3 password chap123
```

```
interface lo0
 ip address 209.165.200.225 255.255.255.252
interface s0/0/0
 ip address 192.168.12.2 255.255.255.252
 encapsulation ppp
 ppp authentication chap
 no shutdown
interface s0/0/1
 ip address 192.168.23.1 255.255.255.252
 clock rate 128000


 no shutdown
 exit
router ospf 1
 router-id 2.2.2.2
 network 192.168.12.0 0.0.0.3 area 0
 network 192.168.23.0 0.0.0.3 area 0
 default-information originate
 exit
ip route 0.0.0.0 0.0.0.0 loopback0
line con 0
 password cisco
 logging synchronous
 login
line vty 0 4
 password cisco
 login
```

**Router R3 Configuration:**

```
hostname R3
enable secret class
no ip domain lookup
banner motd #Unauthorized Access is Prohibited!#
username R2 password chap123
username R3 password chap123


interface g0/1
 ip address 192.168.3.1 255.255.255.0
 no shutdown
interface s0/0/0
 ip address 192.168.13.2 255.255.255.252
 clock rate 128000
 encapsulation ppp
 ppp authentication chap
 no shutdown
```

```
interface s0/0/1
 ip address 192.168.23.2 255.255.255.252
 encapsulation ppp
 ppp authentication chap
 no shutdown
 exit
router ospf 1
 router-id 3.3.3.3

 network 192.168.13.0 0.0.0.3 area 0
 network 192.168.23.0 0.0.0.3 area 0
 passive-interface g0/1
line con 0
 password cisco
 logging synchronous
 login
line vty 0 4
 password cisco
 login
```

### Step 4: Save your running configuration.

## Part 2: Troubleshoot the Data Link Layer

In Part 2, you will use **show** commands to troubleshoot data link layer issues. Be sure to verify settings, such as clock rate, encapsulation, CHAP, and usernames/passwords.

### Step 1: Examine the R1 configuration.

a. Use the **show interfaces** command to determine whether PPP has been established on both serial links.

From the **show interfaces** results for S0/0/0 and S0/0/1, what are possible issues with the PPP links?

____________________________________________________________

____________________________________________________________

Use the **debug ppp authentication** command to view real-time PPP authentication output during troubleshooting.

```
R1# debug ppp authentication
PPP authentication debugging is on
```

b. Use the **show run interface s0/0/0** command to examine the settings on S0/0/0.

Resolve all problems found for S0/0/0. Record the commands used to correct the configuration.

____________________________________________________________

After correcting the issue, what information does the debug output provide?

____________________________________________________________

c. Use the **show run interface s0/0/1** command to examine the settings on S0/0/1.

Resolve all problems found for S0/0/1. Record the commands used to correct the configuration.

____________________________________________________________

____________________________________________________________

After correcting the issue, what information does the debug output provide?

_______________________________________________

_______________________________________________

d. Use the **no debug ppp authentication** or **undebug all** command to turn off the debug PPP output.

e. Use the **show running-config | include username** command to verify the correct username and password configurations.

Resolve all problems found. Record the commands used to correct the configuration.

_______________________________________________

### Step 2: Examine the R2 configuration.

a. Use the **show interfaces** command to determine if PPP has been established on both serial links.

Have all links been established? __________

If the answer is no, which links need to be examined? What are the possible issues?

_______________________________________________

b. Use the **show run interface** command to examine links that have not been established.

Resolve all problems found for the interfaces. Record the commands used to correct the configuration.

_______________________________________________

_______________________________________________

c. Use the **show running-config | include username** command to verify the correct username and password configurations.

Resolve all problems found. Record the commands used to correct the configuration.

_______________________________________________

_______________________________________________

d. Use the **show ppp interface serial** command for the serial interface that you are troubleshooting.

Has the link been established? __________

### Step 3: Examine the R3 configuration.

a. Use the **show interfaces** command to determine whether PPP has been established on both serial links.

Have all links been established? __________

If the answer is no, which links need to be examined? What are the possible issues?

_______________________________________________

b. Using the **show run interface** command to examine on any serial link that has not been established.

Resolve all problems found on the interfaces. Record the commands used to correct the configuration.

____________________________________________________________

c. Use the **show running-config | include username** command to verify the correct username and password configurations.

Resolve all problems found. Record the commands used to correct the configuration.

____________________________________________________________

d. Use the **show interface** command to verify that serial links have been established.

e. Have all PPP links been established?__________

f. Can PC-A ping Lo0? _________

g. Can PC-A ping PC-C? _________

**Note**: It may be necessary to disable the PC firewall for pings between the PCs to succeed.

## Part 3: Troubleshoot the Network Layer

In Part 3, you will verify that Layer 3 connectivity is established on all interfaces by examining IPv4 and OSPF configurations.

### Step 1: Verify that the interfaces listed in the Addressing Table are active and configured with the correct IP address information.

Issue the **show ip interface brief** command on all routers to verify that the interfaces are in an up/up state.

Resolve all problems found. Record the commands used to correct the configuration.

____________________________________________________________

### Step 2: Verify OSPF Routing

Issue the **show ip protocols** command to verify that OSPF is running and that all networks are advertised.

Resolve all problems found. Record the commands used to correct the configuration.

____________________________________________________________

Can PC-A ping PC-C? _______

If connectivity does not exist between all hosts, then continue troubleshooting to resolve any remaining issues.

**Note**: It may be necessary to disable the PC firewall for pings between the PCs to succeed.

## Router Interface Summary Table

| Router Interface Summary | | | | |
|---|---|---|---|---|
| **Router Model** | **Ethernet Interface #1** | **Ethernet Interface #2** | **Serial Interface #1** | **Serial Interface #2** |
| 1800 | Fast Ethernet 0/0 (F0/0) | Fast Ethernet 0/1 (F0/1) | Serial 0/0/0 (S0/0/0) | Serial 0/0/1 (S0/0/1) |
| 1900 | Gigabit Ethernet 0/0 (G0/0) | Gigabit Ethernet 0/1 (G0/1) | Serial 0/0/0 (S0/0/0) | Serial 0/0/1 (S0/0/1) |
| 2801 | Fast Ethernet 0/0 (F0/0) | Fast Ethernet 0/1 (F0/1) | Serial 0/1/0 (S0/1/0) | Serial 0/1/1 (S0/1/1) |
| 2811 | Fast Ethernet 0/0 (F0/0) | Fast Ethernet 0/1 (F0/1) | Serial 0/0/0 (S0/0/0) | Serial 0/0/1 (S0/0/1) |
| 2900 | Gigabit Ethernet 0/0 (G0/0) | Gigabit Ethernet 0/1 (G0/1) | Serial 0/0/0 (S0/0/0) | Serial 0/0/1 (S0/0/1) |

**Note**: To find out how the router is configured, look at the interfaces to identify the type of router and how many interfaces the router has. There is no way to effectively list all the combinations of configurations for each router class. This table includes identifiers for the possible combinations of Ethernet and Serial interfaces in the device. The table does not include any other type of interface, even though a specific router may contain one. An example of this might be an ISDN BRI interface. The string in parenthesis is the legal abbreviation that can be used in Cisco IOS commands to represent the interface.

# 3.5.1.1 Class Activity – PPP Validation

## Objective

Use **show** and **debug** commands to troubleshoot PPP.

## Scenario

Three friends who are enrolled in the Cisco Networking Academy want to check their knowledge of PPP network configuration.

They set up a contest where each person will be tested on configuring PPP with defined PPP scenario requirements and varying options. Each person devises a different configuration scenario.

The next day they get together and test each other's configuration using their PPP scenario requirements.

## Resources

- Packet Tracer software
- Stopwatch or timer

### Step 1: Open Packet Tracer.

a. Create a two-router topology with a serial connection.

b. Include one PC and switch attached to each router.

### Step 2: Complete the scenarios.

a. Start the Scenario 1 configuration.

b. The instructor calls the time when the scenario is completed; all students and groups must stop their configuration work at that time.

c. The instructor checks the validity of the completed scenario configuration.

   1) The devices must be able to successfully ping from one end of the topology to the other.

   2) All scenario options requested must be present in the final topology.

   3) The instructor may ask you to prove your work by choosing different **show** and **debug** commands to display the configuration output.

d. Begin the same process as Scenario 2.

   1) Delete Scenario 1 configurations, but you can re-use the same.

   2) Complete Steps 1 and 2 again using the next scenario's requirements.

# Chapter 4 — Frame Relay

## 4.0.1.2 Class Activity – Emerging WAN Technologies

### Objective

Troubleshoot WAN issues that affect internetwork communications in a small- to medium-sized business network.

### Scenario

As the network administrator, in your small- to medium-sized business, you have already moved from leased-line WAN to Frame Relay connectivity for WAN network communication. You are responsible to keep current with all future network upgrades.

To stay current with emerging and developing technologies, you find that there are some alternate options available for WAN connectivity. Some of these include:

- Frame Relay
- Broadband DSL
- Broadband cable modem
- GigaMAN
- VPN
- MPLS

Because you want to offer the best quality, lowest-cost WAN network service to your company, you decide to research, at least, two emerging and developing technologies. It is your intent to gather information about these two alternate WAN options to intelligently discuss the future goals of your network with your business manager and other network administrators.

### Resources

- Internet access to the World Wide Web
- Presentation software

### Directions

#### Step 1: Choose two of the following emerging and developing WAN technologies:

a. Frame Relay
b. Broadband DSL
c. Broadband cable modem
d. GigaMAN
e. VPN
f. MPLS

#### Step 2: Create a matrix to record information about the two WAN technologies you chose. At a minimum, include:

a. A short description of the technology
b. Physical requirements to set up the technology
   1) Cabling requirements
   2) Network devices necessary to operate the WAN technology
   3) Who provides the network devices necessary to operate the WAN technology
c. Benefits of this type of WAN technology
d. Disadvantages to implementing or changing to this form of WAN technology
e. Costs associated with this type of technology

#### Step 3: Create a five-slide presentation for future use with discussions with your business manager or other network administrators.

# 4.2.2.7 Lab – Configuring Frame Relay and Subinterfaces

## Topology

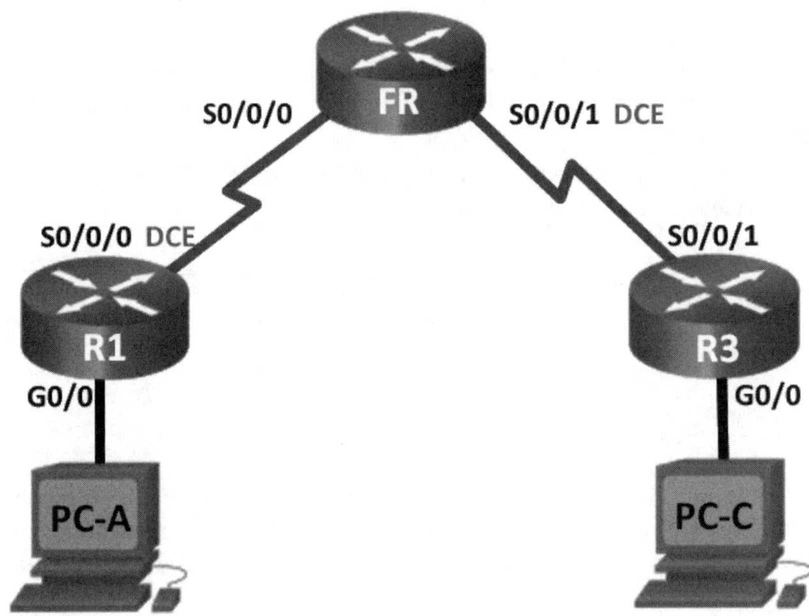

## Addressing Table

| Device | Interface | IPv4 and IPv6 Address | Default Gateway |
|---|---|---|---|
| R1 | G0/0 | 192.168.1.1/24<br>2001:DB8:ACAD:A::1/64<br>FE80::1 link-local | N/A |
| | S0/0/0 (DCE) | 10.1.1.1/30<br>2001:DB8:ACAD:B::1/64<br>FE80::1 link-local | N/A |
| FR | S0/0/0 | N/A | N/A |
| | S0/0/1 (DCE) | N/A | N/A |
| R3 | G0/0 | 192.168.3.1/24<br>2001:DB8:ACAD:C::3/64<br>FE80::3 link-local | N/A |
| | S0/0/1 | 10.1.1.2/30<br>2001:DB8:ACAD:B::3/64<br>FE80::3 link-local | N/A |
| PC-A | NIC | 192.168.1.3/24<br>2001:DB8:ACAD:A::A/64 | 192.168.1.1<br>FE80::1 |
| PC-C | NIC | 192.168.3.3/24<br>2001:DB8:ACAD:C::C/64 | 192.168.3.1<br>FE80::3 |

## Objectives

**Part 1: Build the Network and Configure Basic Device Settings**

**Part 2: Configure a Frame Relay Switch**

**Part 3: Configure Basic Frame Relay**

**Part 4: Troubleshoot Frame Relay**

**Part 5: Configure a Frame Relay Subinterface**

## Background / Scenario

Frame Relay is a high-performance WAN protocol that operates at the physical and data link layers of the OSI reference model. Unlike leased lines, Frame Relay requires only a single access circuit to the Frame Relay provider to communicate with multiple sites that are connected to the same provider.

Frame Relay was one of the most extensively used WAN protocols, primarily because it was relatively inexpensive compared to dedicated lines. In addition, configuring user equipment in a Frame Relay network is fairly simple. With the advent of broadband services such as DSL and cable modem, GigaMAN (point-to-point Ethernet service over fiber-optic cable), VPN, and Multiprotocol Label Switching (MPLS), Frame Relay has become a less desirable solution for accessing the WAN. However, some rural areas do not have access to these alternative solutions and still rely on Frame Relay for connectivity to the WAN.

In this lab, you will configure Frame Relay encapsulation on serial links. You will also configure a router to simulate a Frame Relay switch. You will review Cisco standards and open standards that apply to Frame Relay. You will also configure Frame Relay point-to-point subinterfaces.

**Note**: The routers used with CCNA hands-on labs are Cisco 1941 Integrated Services Routers (ISRs) with Cisco IOS Release 15.2(4)M3 (universalk9 image). Other routers and Cisco IOS versions can be used. Depending on the model and Cisco IOS version, the commands available and output produced might vary from what is shown in the labs. Refer to the Router Interface Summary Table at the end of this lab for the correct interface identifiers.

**Note**: Make sure that the routers have been erased and have no startup configurations. If you are unsure, contact your instructor.

### Required Resources

- 3 Routers (Cisco 1941 with Cisco IOS Release 15.2(4)M3 universal image or comparable)
- 2 PCs (Windows 7, Vista, or XP with terminal emulation program, such as Tera Term)
- Console cables to configure the Cisco IOS devices via the console ports
- Ethernet and serial cables as shown in the topology

## Part 1: Build the Network and Configure Basic Device Settings

In Part 1, you will set up the network topology and configure basic settings on the PC hosts and routers.

### Step 1: Cable the network as shown in the topology.

### Step 2: Initialize and reload the routers as necessary.

### Step 3: Configure basic settings for each router.

a. Disable DNS lookup.

b. Configure device names as shown in the topology.

c. Assign **class** as the privileged EXEC mode password.

d. Assign **cisco** as the console and vty passwords and enable login.

e. Configure **logging synchronous** for the console line.

f. Encrypt the plain text passwords.

g. Configure a MOTD banner to warn users that unauthorized access is prohibited.

h. Set the clocking rate for all DCE serial interfaces to **128000**.

i. Configure the IPv4 and IPv6 addresses listed in the Addressing Table for all interfaces. Do not activate the serial interfaces at this time.

j. Copy the running configuration to the startup configuration.

### Step 4: Configure PC hosts.

Refer to the Addressing Table for PC host address information.

### Step 5: Test connectivity.

At this point, the PCs will not be able to ping each other, but they should be able to ping their default gateway. Test both protocols, IPv4 and IPv6. Verify and troubleshoot if necessary.

## Part 2: Configure a Frame Relay Switch

In Part 2, you will configure a Frame Relay switch. You will create permanent virtual circuits (PVCs) and assign Data Link Connection Identifiers (DLCIs). This configuration creates two PVCs: one from R1 to R3 (DLCI 103), and one from R3 to R1 (DLCI 301).

### Step 1: Configure the FR router as a Frame Relay switch.

The **frame-relay switching** command enables Frame Relay switching globally on a router, allowing it to forward frames based on the incoming DLCI rather than an IP address.

```
FR(config)# frame-relay switching
```

### Step 2: Change the interface encapsulation on S0/0/0.

Change the interface encapsulation type to Frame Relay. Like HDLC or PPP, Frame Relay is a data-link layer protocol that specifies the framing of Layer 2 traffic.

```
FR(config)# interface s0/0/0
FR(config-if)# encapsulation frame-relay
```

### Step 3: Change the interface type to DCE.

Changing the interface type to DCE tells the router to send Local Management Interface (LMI) keepalives and allows Frame Relay route statements to be applied.

**Note**: Frame Relay interface types do not need to match the underlying physical interface type. A physical DTE serial interface can act as a Frame Relay DCE interface, and a physical DCE interface can act as a logical Frame Relay DTE interface.

```
FR(config)# interface s0/0/0
FR(config-if)# frame-relay intf-type dce
```

### Step 4: Configure DLCI.

Configure the router to forward incoming traffic on interface S0/0/0 with DLCI 103 to S0/0/1 with an output of DLCI of 301.

```
FR(config-if)# frame-relay route 103 interface s0/0/1 301
FR(config-if)# no shutdown
```

### Step 5: Configure Frame Relay on S0/0/1.

```
FR(config)# interface s0/0/1
FR(config-if)# encapsulation frame-relay
FR(config-if)# frame-relay intf-type dce
FR(config-if)# frame-relay route 301 interface s0/0/0 103
FR(config-if)# no shutdown
```

### Step 6: Verify Frame Relay configuration.

a. Use the **show frame-relay pvc** command to verify that Frame Relay is configured correctly.

```
FR# show frame-relay pvc

PVC Statistics for interface Serial0/0/0 (Frame Relay DCE)
```

```
              Active     Inactive      Deleted       Static
  Local          0           0            0             0
  Switched       0           1            0             0
  Unused         0           0            0             0

DLCI = 103, DLCI USAGE = SWITCHED, PVC STATUS = INACTIVE, INTERFACE = Serial0/0/0

  input pkts 0             output pkts 0             in bytes 0
  out bytes 0              dropped pkts 0            in pkts dropped 0
  out pkts dropped 0                out bytes dropped 0
  in FECN pkts 0           in BECN pkts 0            out FECN pkts 0
  out BECN pkts 0          in DE pkts 0              out DE pkts 0
  out bcast pkts 0         out bcast bytes 0
  30 second input rate 0 bits/sec, 0 packets/sec
  30 second output rate 0 bits/sec, 0 packets/sec
  switched pkts 0
  Detailed packet drop counters:
  no out intf 0            out intf down 0           no out PVC 0
  in PVC down 0            out PVC down 0            pkt too big 0
  shaping Q full 0         pkt above DE 0            policing drop 0
  connected to interface Serial0/0/1 301
  pvc create time 00:00:53, last time pvc status changed 00:00:53

PVC Statistics for interface Serial0/0/1 (Frame Relay DCE)

              Active     Inactive      Deleted       Static
  Local          0           0            0             0
  Switched       0           1            0             0
  Unused         0           0            0             0

DLCI = 301, DLCI USAGE = SWITCHED, PVC STATUS = INACTIVE, INTERFACE = Serial0/0/1

  input pkts 0             output pkts 0             in bytes 0
  out bytes 0              dropped pkts 0            in pkts dropped 0
  out pkts dropped 0                out bytes dropped 0
  in FECN pkts 0           in BECN pkts 0            out FECN pkts 0
  out BECN pkts 0          in DE pkts 0              out DE pkts 0
  out bcast pkts 0         out bcast bytes 0
  30 second input rate 0 bits/sec, 0 packets/sec
  30 second output rate 0 bits/sec, 0 packets/sec
  switched pkts 0
  Detailed packet drop counters:
  no out intf 0            out intf down 0           no out PVC 0
  in PVC down 0            out PVC down 0            pkt too big 0
  shaping Q full 0         pkt above DE 0            policing drop 0
  connected to interface Serial0/0/0 103
  pvc create time 00:00:16, last time pvc status changed 00:00:16
```

b. Issue the **show frame-relay route** command. This is the Layer 2 route that Frame Relay traffic takes through the network. (Do not confuse this with Layer 3 IP routing.)

```
FR# show frame-relay route
```

```
Input Intf      Input Dlci     Output Intf     Output Dlci     Status
Serial0/0/0     103            Serial0/0/1     301             inactive
Serial0/0/1     301            Serial0/0/0     103             inactive
```

## Part 3: Configure Basic Frame Relay

In Part 3, you will configure Frame Relay on routers R1 and R3. After Frame Relay is configured, you will enable the EIGRP routing protocol to provide end-to-end connectivity.

### Step 1: Configure R1 for Frame Relay.

Inverse ARP allows distant ends of a Frame Relay link to discover each other dynamically, and provides a dynamic method of mapping IP addresses to DLCIs. Although Inverse ARP is useful, it is not always reliable. The best practice is to map IP addresses to DLCIs statically and disable Inverse ARP.

a. Change the encapsulation on S0/0/0 to Frame Relay.

```
R1(config)# interface s0/0/0
R1(config-if)# encapsulation frame-relay
```

b. Use the **no frame-relay inverse-arp** command to disable Inverse ARP.

```
R1(config)# interface s0/0/0
R1(config-if)# no frame-relay inverse-arp
```

c. Use the **frame-relay map** command to map an IP address to a DLCI statically. In addition to mapping an IP to a DLCI, Cisco IOS software allows several other Layer 3 protocol addresses to be mapped. In the following command, the **broadcast** keyword sends any multicast or broadcast traffic destined for this link over the DLCI. Most routing protocols require the **broadcast** keyword to function properly over Frame Relay. You can use the **broadcast** keyword on multiple DLCIs on the same interface. The traffic is replicated to all PVCs.

**Note**: The IPv6 Frame Relay map to a global unicast address does not include the **broadcast** keyword. However, the **broadcast** keyword is used in the mapping to the link-local address. IPv6 routing protocols use link-local addresses for multicast routing updates; therefore, only the link-local address map requires the **broadcast** keyword to forward multicast packets.

```
R1(config)# interface s0/0/0
R1(config-if)# frame-relay map ip 10.1.1.2 103 broadcast
R1(config-if)# frame-relay map ipv6 2001:db8:acad:b::3 103
R1(config-if)# frame-relay map ipv6 fe80::3 103 broadcast
```

d. For the router to ping its own interface, the DLCI must be created to map to the local interface.

```
R1(config)# interface s0/0/0
R1(config-if)# frame-relay map ip 10.1.1.1 103
R1(config-if)# frame-relay map ipv6 2001:db8:acad:b::1 103
```

e. Use the **no shutdown** command to activate S0/0/0.

```
R1(config-if)# no shutdown
```

### Step 2: Configure R3 for Frame Relay.

```
R3(config)# interface s0/0/1
R3(config-if)# encapsulation frame-relay
R3(config-if)# no frame-relay inverse-arp
R3(config-if)# frame-relay map ip 10.1.1.1 301 broadcast
R3(config-if)# frame-relay map ipv6 2001:db8:acad:b::1 301
R3(config-if)# frame-relay map ipv6 fe80::1 301 broadcast
```

```
R3(config-if)# frame-relay map ip 10.1.1.2 301
R3(config-if)# frame-relay map ipv6 2001:db8:acad:b::3 301
R3(config-if)# no shutdown
```

Why is the **no shutdown** command used after the **no frame-relay inverse-arp** command?

_______________________________________________

_______________________________________________

_______________________________________________

### Step 3: Verify that Frame Relay is active.

a. You should now be able to ping R3 from R1. It may take several seconds after bringing up the interfaces for the PVCs to become active.

```
R1# ping 10.1.1.2
Type escape sequence to abort.
Sending 5, 100-byte ICMP Echos to 10.1.1.2, timeout is 2 seconds:
!!!!!
Success rate is 100 percent (5/5), round-trip min/avg/max = 28/30/40 ms
R1# ping 2001:db8:acad:b::3
Type escape sequence to abort.
Sending 5, 100-byte ICMP Echos to 2001:DB8:ACAD:B::3, timeout is 2 seconds:
!!!!!
Success rate is 100 percent (5/5), round-trip min/avg/max = 28/28/28 ms
```

b. Ping R1 from R3.

```
R3# ping 10.1.1.1
Type escape sequence to abort.
Sending 5, 100-byte ICMP Echos to 10.1.1.1, timeout is 2 seconds:
!!!!!
Success rate is 100 percent (5/5), round-trip min/avg/max = 28/28/28 ms
R3# ping 2001:db8:acad:b::1
Type escape sequence to abort.
Sending 5, 100-byte ICMP Echos to 2001:DB8:ACAD:B::1, timeout is 2 seconds:
!!!!!
Success rate is 100 percent (5/5), round-trip min/avg/max = 24/26/28 ms
```

c. Issue the **show frame-relay pvc** command to display PVC status information on R1 and R3.

```
R1# show frame-relay pvc

PVC Statistics for interface Serial0/0/0 (Frame Relay DTE)

              Active     Inactive      Deleted       Static
  Local          1            0            0            0
  Switched       0            0            0            0
  Unused         0            0            0            0
```

```
DLCI = 103, DLCI USAGE = LOCAL, PVC STATUS = ACTIVE, INTERFACE = Serial0/0/0

  input pkts 22            output pkts 154          in bytes 2240
  out bytes 10860          dropped pkts 0           in pkts dropped 0
  out pkts dropped 0                out bytes dropped 0
  in FECN pkts 0           in BECN pkts 0           out FECN pkts 0
  out BECN pkts 0          in DE pkts 0             out DE pkts 0
  out bcast pkts 134       out bcast bytes 8780
  5 minute input rate 0 bits/sec, 0 packets/sec
  5 minute output rate 0 bits/sec, 0 packets/sec
  pvc create time 01:59:40, last time pvc status changed 01:55:14

R3# show frame-relay pvc

PVC Statistics for interface Serial0/0/1 (Frame Relay DTE)

              Active     Inactive      Deleted       Static
  Local          1            0            0            0
  Switched       0            0            0            0
  Unused         0            0            0            0

DLCI = 301, DLCI USAGE = LOCAL, PVC STATUS = ACTIVE, INTERFACE = Serial0/0/1

  input pkts 158           output pkts 22           in bytes 11156
  out bytes 2240           dropped pkts 0           in pkts dropped 0
  out pkts dropped 0                out bytes dropped 0
  in FECN pkts 0           in BECN pkts 0           out FECN pkts 0
  out BECN pkts 0          in DE pkts 0             out DE pkts 0
  out bcast pkts 2         out bcast bytes 160
  5 minute input rate 0 bits/sec, 0 packets/sec
  5 minute output rate 0 bits/sec, 0 packets/sec
  pvc create time 01:57:20, last time pvc status changed 01:56:19
```

d. Issue the **show frame-relay route** command on FR to verify that status of the Frame Relay map statements.

```
FR# show frame-relay route
Input Intf      Input Dlci      Output Intf     Output Dlci     Status
Serial0/0/0     103             Serial0/0/1     301             active
Serial0/0/1     301             Serial0/0/0     103             active
```

e. Issue the **show frame-relay map** command on R1 and R3 to display a summary of the static and dynamic mappings of Layer 3 addresses to DLCIs. Because Inverse ARP has been turned off, there are only static maps.

```
R1# show frame-relay map
Serial0/0/0 (up): ipv6 FE80::3 dlci 103(0x67,0x1870), static,
              broadcast,
              CISCO, status defined, active
Serial0/0/0 (up): ipv6 2001:DB8:ACAD:B::1 dlci 103(0x67,0x1870), static,
              CISCO, status defined, active
Serial0/0/0 (up): ip 10.1.1.1 dlci 103(0x67,0x1870), static,
              CISCO, status defined, active
Serial0/0/0 (up): ipv6 2001:DB8:ACAD:B::3 dlci 103(0x67,0x1870), static,
```

```
              CISCO, status defined, active
Serial0/0/0 (up): ip 10.1.1.2 dlci 103(0x67,0x1870), static,
              broadcast,
              CISCO, status defined, active

R3# show frame-relay map
Serial0/0/1 (up): ipv6 FE80::1 dlci 301(0x12D,0x48D0), static,
              broadcast,
              CISCO, status defined, active
Serial0/0/1 (up): ipv6 2001:DB8:ACAD:B::3 dlci 301(0x12D,0x48D0), static,
              CISCO, status defined, active
Serial0/0/1 (up): ip 10.1.1.2 dlci 301(0x12D,0x48D0), static,
              CISCO, status defined, active
Serial0/0/1 (up): ipv6 2001:DB8:ACAD:B::1 dlci 301(0x12D,0x48D0), static,
              CISCO, status defined, active
Serial0/0/1 (up): ip 10.1.1.1 dlci 301(0x12D,0x48D0), static,
              broadcast,
              CISCO, status defined, active
```

**Note**: The FR router acts as a Layer 2 device, so there is no need to map Layer 3 addresses to Layer 2 DLCIs.

### Step 4: Configure EIGRP on R1 and R3.

a. Enable IPv6 routing on R1 and R3.

b. Using AS 1, enable EIGRP for IPv4 and IPv6 on R1 and R3 for all networks. Set the router ID for R1 as 1.1.1.1 and 3.3.3.3 for R3.

### Step 5: Verify end-to-end connectivity.

Ping PC-C from PC-A. If your pings were unsuccessful, troubleshoot until you have end-to-end connectivity.

**Note**: It may be necessary to disable the PC firewall for pings to be successful.

## Part 4: Troubleshoot Frame Relay

In Part 4, you will break the Frame Relay connection established earlier and use some tools to troubleshoot Frame Relay. A variety of tools are available for troubleshooting Frame Relay connectivity issues.

### Step 1: Debug Local Management Interface (LMI).

a. Issue the **debug frame-relay lmi** command on R1. The output gives detailed information on all LMI data. Keepalives are sent every 10 seconds by default, so you may have to wait until you see any output. The output shows an outgoing LMI packet with a sequence number of 50. The last LMI message received from FR had a sequence number of 49. The output is also showing an incoming LMI message from FR to R1 with a sequence number of 50. DLCI 103 is the only DLCI on this link, and it is currently active.

```
R1# debug frame-relay lmi
Frame Relay LMI debugging is on
Displaying all Frame Relay LMI data
R1#
*Jun 26 18:28:45.922: Serial0/0/0(out): StEnq, myseq 50, yourseen 49, DTE up
*Jun 26 18:28:45.922: datagramstart = 0xC318D54, datagramsize = 13
*Jun 26 18:28:45.922: FR encap = 0xFCF10309
```

```
*Jun 26 18:28:45.922: 00 75 01 01 01 03 02 32 31
*Jun 26 18:28:45.922:
*Jun 26 18:28:45.922: Serial0/0/0(in): Status, myseq 50, pak size 13
*Jun 26 18:28:45.922: RT IE 1, length 1, type 1
*Jun 26 18:28:45.922: KA IE 3, length 2, yourseq 50, myseq 50
*Jun 26 18:28:45.922: PVC IE 0x7 , length 0x6 , dlci 103 , status 0x2 , bw 0
```

b. Issue the **undebug all** command to turn off debugging.

**Note**: This command can be abbreviated to **u all**. This is useful to know when debug information is flooding the screen.

```
R1# undebug all
All possible debugging has been turned off
```

### Step 2: Remove the IPv4 frame map from R1.

a. Issue the **no frame-relay map** command to remove the IPv4 frame map on R1.

```
R1(config)# interface s0/0/0
R1(config-if)# no frame-relay map ip 10.1.1.2 103 broadcast
```

b. Issue the **debug ip icmp** command on R1.

```
R1# debug ip icmp
ICMP packet debugging is on
```

c. Ping R1 from R3. Pings should not be successful. However, debug messages on R1 show that the ICMP packets from R3 are reaching R1.

**Note**: You should see console messages reporting the EIGRP adjacency going up and down. This is sometimes called flapping.

```
R3# ping 10.1.1.1
Type escape sequence to abort.
Sending 5, 100-byte ICMP Echos to 10.1.1.1, timeout is 2 seconds:
.....
Success rate is 0 percent (0/5)

R1#
*Jun 26 20:12:35.693: ICMP: echo reply sent, src 10.1.1.1, dst 10.1.1.2, topology
BASE, dscp 0 topoid 0
R1#
*Jun 26 20:12:37.689: ICMP: echo reply sent, src 10.1.1.1, dst 10.1.1.2, topology
BASE, dscp 0 topoid 0
R1#
*Jun 26 20:12:39.689: ICMP: echo reply sent, src 10.1.1.1, dst 10.1.1.2, topology
BASE, dscp 0 topoid 0
R1#
*Jun 26 20:12:41.689: ICMP: echo reply sent, src 10.1.1.1, dst 10.1.1.2, topology
BASE, dscp 0 topoid 0
R1#
*Jun 26 20:12:43.689: ICMP: echo reply sent, src 10.1.1.1, dst 10.1.1.2, topology
BASE, dscp 0 topoid 0
```

Why does the ping fail?

____________________________________________________________

____________________________________________________________

d. Issue the **show frame-relay map** command on R1. The IPv4 map for R3 is missing from the list.

```
R1# show frame-relay map
Serial0/0/0 (up): ipv6 FE80::3 dlci 103(0x67,0x1870), static,
              broadcast,
              CISCO, status defined, active
Serial0/0/0 (up): ipv6 2001:DB8:ACAD:B::1 dlci 103(0x67,0x1870), static,
              CISCO, status defined, active
Serial0/0/0 (up): ip 10.1.1.1 dlci 103(0x67,0x1870), static,
              CISCO, status defined, active
Serial0/0/0 (up): ipv6 2001:DB8:ACAD:B::3 dlci 103(0x67,0x1870), static,
              CISCO, status defined, active
```

e. Issue the **undebug all** command to turn off debugging on R1.

```
R1# undebug all
All possible debugging has been turned off
```

f. Re-apply the **frame-relay map ip** command to S0/0/0 on R1, but without using the **broadcast** keyword.

```
R1(config)# interface s0/0/0
R1(config-if)# frame-relay map ip 10.1.1.2 103
```

g. Ping R1 from R3. Pings should be successful, but the EIGRP adjacency continues to flap. It may take a few minutes between each message because of the EIGRP timers.

```
R3# ping 10.1.1.1
Type escape sequence to abort.
Sending 5, 100-byte ICMP Echos to 10.1.1.1, timeout is 2 seconds:
!!!!!
Success rate is 100 percent (5/5), round-trip min/avg/max = 28/28/28 ms

R1(config-if)#
*Jun 26 20:25:10.871: %DUAL-5-NBRCHANGE: EIGRP-IPv4 1: Neighbor 10.1.1.2 (Serial0/0/0)
is down: Interface PEER-TERMINATION received
*Jun 26 20:28:13.673: %DUAL-5-NBRCHANGE: EIGRP-IPv4 1: Neighbor 10.1.1.2 (Serial0/0/0)
is up: new adjacency
R1(config-if)#
*Jun 26 20:31:18.185: %DUAL-5-NBRCHANGE: EIGRP-IPv4 1: Neighbor 10.1.1.2 (Serial0/0/0)
is down: retry limit exceeded
R1(config-if)#
*Jun 26 20:32:00.977: %DUAL-5-NBRCHANGE: EIGRP-IPv4 1: Neighbor 10.1.1.2 (Serial0/0/0)
is up: new adjacency
R1(config-if)#
*Jun 26 20:35:05.489: %DUAL-5-NBRCHANGE: EIGRP-IPv4 1: Neighbor 10.1.1.2 (Serial0/0/0)
is down: retry limit exceeded
```

Why does the EIGRP adjacency continue to flap?

_______________________________________________

h. Replace the Frame Relay map statement and include the **broadcast** keyword this time.

```
R1(config-if)# frame-relay map ip 10.1.1.2 103 broadcast
```

i. Verify that the full routing table is restored and that you have end-to-end connectivity.

## Step 3: Change the Frame Relay encapsulation type.

Cisco IOS software supports two types of Frame Relay encapsulation: the default Cisco encapsulation and the standards-based IETF encapsulation.

a. Change the Frame Relay encapsulation on S0/0/1 on R3 to IETF.

```
R3(config)# interface s0/0/1
R3(config-if)# encapsulation frame-relay ietf
```

b. Issue the **show interfaces s0/0/1** command on R3 and FR. Even though the encapsulation is different on each interface, the link is still active. This is because Cisco routers understand both types of incoming frames. However, if you have routers from different vendors and you are using Frame Relay, then the IETF standard must be used.

```
R3# show interfaces s0/0/1
Serial0/0/1 is up, line protocol is up
  Hardware is WIC MBRD Serial
  Internet address is 10.1.1.2/30
  MTU 1500 bytes, BW 1544 Kbit/sec, DLY 20000 usec,
     reliability 255/255, txload 1/255, rxload 1/255
  Encapsulation FRAME-RELAY IETF, loopback not set
  Keepalive set (10 sec)
  LMI enq sent  1898, LMI stat recvd 1900, LMI upd recvd 0, DTE LMI up
<output omitted>

FR# show interfaces s0/0/1
Serial0/0/1 is up, line protocol is up
  Hardware is WIC MBRD Serial
  MTU 1500 bytes, BW 1544 Kbit/sec, DLY 20000 usec,
     reliability 255/255, txload 1/255, rxload 1/255
  Encapsulation FRAME-RELAY, loopback not set
  Keepalive set (10 sec)
  LMI enq sent  0, LMI stat recvd 0, LMI upd recvd 0
```

c. Reset the R3 Frame Relay encapsulation back to Cisco (the default).

```
R3(config)# interface s0/0/1
R3(config-if)# encapsulation frame-relay
```

## Step 4: Change the LMI type.

a. Issue the **frame-relay lmi-type ansi** command on interface S0/0/1 on R3.

```
R3(config-if)# frame-relay lmi-type ansi
```

b. After at least 60 seconds, issue the **show interfaces s0/0/1** command on R3. When 60 seconds have passed, the interface changes its state to up, then down, because R3 is expecting ANSI LMI, and FR is sending Cisco LMI.

```
R3# show interfaces s0/0/1
Serial0/0/1 is up, line protocol is down
  Hardware is WIC MBRD Serial
  Internet address is 10.1.1.2/30
  MTU 1500 bytes, BW 1544 Kbit/sec, DLY 20000 usec,
     reliability 255/255, txload 1/255, rxload 1/255
  Encapsulation FRAME-RELAY, loopback not set
  Keepalive set (10 sec)
  LMI enq sent  2157, LMI stat recvd 2136, LMI upd recvd 0, DTE LMI down
```

```
  LMI enq recvd 0, LMI stat sent  0, LMI upd sent  0
  LMI DLCI 0  LMI type is ANSI Annex D  frame relay DTE  segmentation inactive
  FR SVC disabled, LAPF state down
  Broadcast queue 0/64, broadcasts sent/dropped 733/0, interface broadcast
<output omitted>
```

c. On R3, issue the **show frame-relay lmi** command to display LMI information, including LMI type, number of timeouts, and the amount of time since the last full update.

```
R3# show frame-relay lmi

LMI Statistics for interface Serial0/0/1 (Frame Relay DTE) LMI TYPE = ANSI
  Invalid Unnumbered info 0              Invalid Prot Disc 0
  Invalid dummy Call Ref 0               Invalid Msg Type 0
  Invalid Status Message 0               Invalid Lock Shift 0
  Invalid Information ID 0               Invalid Report IE Len 0
  Invalid Report Request 0               Invalid Keep IE Len 0
  Num Status Enq. Sent 2158              Num Status msgs Rcvd 2136
  Num Update Status Rcvd 0               Num Status Timeouts 23
  Last Full Status Req 00:00:05          Last Full Status Rcvd 00:04:35
```

d. On R3, issue the **debug frame-relay lmi** command. The LMI packets no longer display in pairs. While all outgoing LMI messages are logged, no incoming messages display because R3 is expecting ANSI LMI, and FR is sending Cisco LMI.

```
R3# debug frame-relay lmi
Frame Relay LMI debugging is on
Displaying all Frame Relay LMI data
R3#
*Jun 26 21:49:10.829: Serial0/0/1(out): StEnq, myseq 104, yourseen 0, DTE down
*Jun 26 21:49:10.829: datagramstart = 0xC313554, datagramsize = 14
*Jun 26 21:49:10.829: FR encap = 0x00010308
*Jun 26 21:49:10.829: 00 75 95 01 01 00 03 02 68 00
*Jun 26 21:49:10.829:
R3#
*Jun 26 21:49:20.829: Serial0/0/1(out): StEnq, myseq 105, yourseen 0, DTE down
*Jun 26 21:49:20.829: datagramstart = 0xC317554, datagramsize = 14
*Jun 26 21:49:20.829: FR encap = 0x00010308
*Jun 26 21:49:20.829: 00 75 95 01 01 00 03 02 69 00
*Jun 26 21:49:20.829:
```

e. Restore the LMI type back to Cisco on R3. Notice that the debug messages change after you issue this command. The LMI sequence number has been reset to 1. R3 began to understand the LMI messages coming in from FR. After R3 and FR have successfully exchanged LMI messages, the interface changed state to up.

```
R3(config)# interface s0/0/1
R3(config-if)# frame-relay lmi-type cisco
R3(config-if)#
*Jun 26 21:51:20.829: Serial0/0/1(out): StEnq, myseq 117, yourseen 0, DTE down
*Jun 26 21:51:20.829: datagramstart = 0xC31F254, datagramsize = 14
*Jun 26 21:51:20.829: FR encap = 0x00010308
*Jun 26 21:51:20.829: 00 75 95 01 01 00 03 02 75 00
*Jun 26 21:51:20.829:
R3(config-if)#
*Jun 26 21:51:30.829: Serial0/0/1(out): StEnq, myseq 1, yourseen 0, DTE down
```

```
*Jun 26 21:51:30.829: datagramstart = 0xC31F3D4, datagramsize = 13
*Jun 26 21:51:30.829: FR encap = 0xFCF10309
*Jun 26 21:51:30.829: 00 75 01 01 00 03 02 01 00
*Jun 26 21:51:30.829:
*Jun 26 21:51:30.829: Serial0/0/1(in): Status, myseq 1, pak size 21
*Jun 26 21:51:30.829: RT IE 1, length 1, type 0
*Jun 26 21:51:30.829: KA IE 3, length 2, yourseq 1 , myseq 1
*Jun 26 21:51:30.829: PVC IE 0x7 , length 0x6 , dlci 301, stat
R3(config-if)#us 0x2 , bw 0
R3(config-if)#
*Jun 26 21:51:40.829: Serial0/0/1(out): StEnq, myseq 2, yourseen 1, DTE down
*Jun 26 21:51:40.829: datagramstart = 0xC313B54, datagramsize = 13
*Jun 26 21:51:40.829: FR encap = 0xFCF10309
*Jun 26 21:51:40.829: 00 75 01 01 01 03 02 02 01
*Jun 26 21:51:40.829:
*Jun 26 21:51:40.829: Serial0/0/1(in): Status, myseq 2, pak size 21
*Jun 26 21:51:40.829: RT IE 1, length 1, type 0
*Jun 26 21:51:40.829: KA IE 3, length 2, yourseq 2 , myseq 2
*Jun 26 21:51:40.829: PVC IE 0x7 , length 0x6 , dlci 301, stat
R3(config-if)#us 0x2 , bw 0
*Jun 26 21:51:51.829: %LINEPROTO-5-UPDOWN: Line protocol on Interface
Serial0/0/1, changed state to up
R3(config-if)#
```

f. Issue the **undebug all** command to end debugging.

```
R3# undebug all
All possible debugging has been turned off
```

## Part 5: Configure a Frame Relay Subinterface

Frame Relay supports two types of subinterfaces: point-to-point and point-to-multipoint. Point-to-multipoint subinterfaces support non-broadcast multiaccess topologies. For example, a hub and spoke topology would use a point-to-multipoint subinterface. In Part 5, you will create a point-to-point subinterface.

### Step 1: On the FR router, create new PVCs between R1 and R3.

```
FR(config)# interface s0/0/0
FR(config-if)# frame-relay route 113 interface s0/0/1 311
FR(config-if)# interface s0/0/1
FR(config-if)# frame-relay route 311 interface s0/0/0 113
```

### Step 2: Create and configure a point-to-point subinterface on R1 and R3.

**Note**: Frame Relay encapsulation must be specified on the physical interface before subinterfaces can be created.

a. Create subinterface 113 as a point-to-point interface on R1.

```
R1(config)# interface s0/0/0.113 point-to-point
R1(config-subif)# ip address 10.1.1.5 255.255.255.252
R1(config-subif)# ipv6 address 2001:db8:acad:d::1/64
R1(config-subif)# ipv6 address fe80::1 link-local
R1(config-subif)# frame-relay interface-dlci 113
R1(config-fr-dlci)#
```

b. Create subinterface 311 as a point-to-point subinterface on R3.

```
R3(config)# interface s0/0/1.311 point-to-point
R3(config-subif)# ip address 10.1.1.6 255.255.255.252
R3(config-subif)# ipv6 address 2001:db8:acad:d::3/64
R3(config-subif)# ipv6 address fe80::3 link-local
R3(config-subif)# frame-relay interface-dlci 311
R3(config-fr-dlci)#
```

c. Verify connectivity.

```
R1# ping 10.1.1.6
Type escape sequence to abort.
Sending 5, 100-byte ICMP Echos to 10.1.1.6, timeout is 2 seconds:
!!!!!
Success rate is 100 percent (5/5), round-trip min/avg/max = 28/28/28 ms
R1# ping 2001:db8:acad:d::3
Type escape sequence to abort.
Sending 5, 100-byte ICMP Echos to 2001:DB8:ACAD:D::3, timeout is 2 seconds:
!!!!!
Success rate is 100 percent (5/5), round-trip min/avg/max = 28/28/28 ms

R3# ping 10.1.1.5
Type escape sequence to abort.
Sending 5, 100-byte ICMP Echos to 10.1.1.5, timeout is 2 seconds:
!!!!!
Success rate is 100 percent (5/5), round-trip min/avg/max = 28/28/28 ms
R3# ping 2001:db8:acad:d::1
Type escape sequence to abort.
Sending 5, 100-byte ICMP Echos to 2001:DB8:ACAD:D::1, timeout is 2 seconds:
!!!!!
Success rate is 100 percent (5/5), round-trip min/avg/max = 28/28/28 ms
```

d. Issue the **show frame-relay pvc** command on R1 and R3 to display the PVC status.

```
R1# show frame-relay pvc

PVC Statistics for interface Serial0/0/0 (Frame Relay DTE)

              Active     Inactive      Deleted       Static
  Local          2            0            0            0
  Switched       0            0            0            0
  Unused         0            0            0            0

DLCI = 103, DLCI USAGE = LOCAL, PVC STATUS = ACTIVE, INTERFACE = Serial0/0/0

  input pkts 1170          output pkts 1408         in bytes 92566
  out bytes 105327         dropped pkts 0           in pkts dropped 0
  out pkts dropped 0                out bytes dropped 0
  in FECN pkts 0           in BECN pkts 0           out FECN pkts 0
  out BECN pkts 0          in DE pkts 0             out DE pkts 0
  out bcast pkts 1160      out bcast bytes 89034
  5 minute input rate 0 bits/sec, 0 packets/sec
  5 minute output rate 0 bits/sec, 0 packets/sec
  pvc create time 07:53:13, last time pvc status changed 00:35:58
```

```
DLCI = 113, DLCI USAGE = LOCAL, PVC STATUS = ACTIVE, INTERFACE = Serial0/0/0.113

  input pkts 86            output pkts 494          in bytes 20916
  out bytes 45208          dropped pkts 0           in pkts dropped 0
  out pkts dropped 0                out bytes dropped 0
  in FECN pkts 0           in BECN pkts 0           out FECN pkts 0
  out BECN pkts 0          in DE pkts 0             out DE pkts 0
  out bcast pkts 464       out bcast bytes 42088
  5 minute input rate 0 bits/sec, 0 packets/sec
  5 minute output rate 0 bits/sec, 0 packets/sec
  pvc create time 00:35:58, last time pvc status changed 00:35:58

R3# show frame-relay pvc

PVC Statistics for interface Serial0/0/1 (Frame Relay DTE)

              Active     Inactive      Deleted       Static
  Local          2           0             0             0
  Switched       0           0             0             0
  Unused         0           0             0             0

DLCI = 301, DLCI USAGE = LOCAL, PVC STATUS = ACTIVE, INTERFACE = Serial0/0/1

  input pkts 1406          output pkts 1176         in bytes 105143
  out bytes 93110          dropped pkts 0           in pkts dropped 0
  out pkts dropped 0                out bytes dropped 0
  in FECN pkts 0           in BECN pkts 0           out FECN pkts 0
  out BECN pkts 0          in DE pkts 0             out DE pkts 0
  out bcast pkts 1038      out bcast bytes 80878
  5 minute input rate 0 bits/sec, 0 packets/sec
  5 minute output rate 0 bits/sec, 0 packets/sec
  pvc create time 07:51:07, last time pvc status changed 00:37:16

DLCI = 311, DLCI USAGE = LOCAL, PVC STATUS = ACTIVE, INTERFACE = Serial0/0/1.311

  input pkts 513           output pkts 114          in bytes 47072
  out bytes 30360          dropped pkts 0           in pkts dropped 0
  out pkts dropped 0                out bytes dropped 0
  in FECN pkts 0           in BECN pkts 0           out FECN pkts 0
  out BECN pkts 0          in DE pkts 0             out DE pkts 0
  out bcast pkts 74        out bcast bytes 26200
  5 minute input rate 0 bits/sec, 0 packets/sec
  5 minute output rate 0 bits/sec, 0 packets/sec
  pvc create time 01:11:06, last time pvc status changed 00:37:16
```

e. Issue the **show frame-relay route** command on FR to verify the status of the Frame Relay map statements.

```
FR# show frame-relay route
Input Intf      Input Dlci      Output Intf     Output Dlci     Status
Serial0/0/0     103             Serial0/0/1     301             active
Serial0/0/0     113             Serial0/0/1     311             active
```

```
Serial0/0/1     301             Serial0/0/0     103             active
Serial0/0/1     311             Serial0/0/0     113             active
```

f. Issue the **show frame-relay map** command on R1 and R3 to verify the status of the Frame Relay map statements.

```
R1# show frame-relay map
Serial0/0/0 (up): ip 10.1.1.2 dlci 103(0x67,0x1870), static,
              broadcast,
              CISCO, status defined, active
Serial0/0/0 (up): ipv6 FE80::3 dlci 103(0x67,0x1870), static,
              broadcast,
              CISCO, status defined, active
Serial0/0/0 (up): ipv6 2001:DB8:ACAD:B::1 dlci 103(0x67,0x1870), static,
              CISCO, status defined, active
Serial0/0/0 (up): ip 10.1.1.1 dlci 103(0x67,0x1870), static,
              CISCO, status defined, active
Serial0/0/0 (up): ipv6 2001:DB8:ACAD:B::3 dlci 103(0x67,0x1870), static,
              CISCO, status defined, active
Serial0/0/0.113 (up): point-to-point dlci, dlci 113(0x71,0x1C10), broadcast
          status defined, active

R3# show frame-relay map
Serial0/0/1 (up): ipv6 FE80::1 dlci 301(0x12D,0x48D0), static,
              broadcast,
              CISCO, status defined, active
Serial0/0/1 (up): ipv6 2001:DB8:ACAD:B::3 dlci 301(0x12D,0x48D0), static,
              CISCO, status defined, active
Serial0/0/1 (up): ip 10.1.1.2 dlci 301(0x12D,0x48D0), static,
              CISCO, status defined, active
Serial0/0/1 (up): ipv6 2001:DB8:ACAD:B::1 dlci 301(0x12D,0x48D0), static,
              CISCO, status defined, active
Serial0/0/1 (up): ip 10.1.1.1 dlci 301(0x12D,0x48D0), static,
              broadcast,
              CISCO, status defined, active
Serial0/0/1.311 (up): point-to-point dlci, dlci 311(0x137,0x4C70), broadcast
          status defined, active
```

## Reflection

1. What is a PVC and how is it used?

_______________________________________________

_______________________________________________

_______________________________________________

2. What is the purpose of a DLCI?

_______________________________________________

3. What purpose does the Local Management Interface (LMI) serve in a Frame Relay network?

_______________________________________________________________________________

_______________________________________________________________________________

_______________________________________________________________________________

_______________________________________________________________________________

4. Why would you use subinterfaces with Frame Relay?

_______________________________________________________________________________

_______________________________________________________________________________

_______________________________________________________________________________

_______________________________________________________________________________

## Router Interface Summary Table

| Router Interface Summary | | | | |
|---|---|---|---|---|
| **Router Model** | **Ethernet Interface #1** | **Ethernet Interface #2** | **Serial Interface #1** | **Serial Interface #2** |
| 1800 | Fast Ethernet 0/0 (F0/0) | Fast Ethernet 0/1 (F0/1) | Serial 0/0/0 (S0/0/0) | Serial 0/0/1 (S0/0/1) |
| 1900 | Gigabit Ethernet 0/0 (G0/0) | Gigabit Ethernet 0/1 (G0/1) | Serial 0/0/0 (S0/0/0) | Serial 0/0/1 (S0/0/1) |
| 2801 | Fast Ethernet 0/0 (F0/0) | Fast Ethernet 0/1 (F0/1) | Serial 0/1/0 (S0/1/0) | Serial 0/1/1 (S0/1/1) |
| 2811 | Fast Ethernet 0/0 (F0/0) | Fast Ethernet 0/1 (F0/1) | Serial 0/0/0 (S0/0/0) | Serial 0/0/1 (S0/0/1) |
| 2900 | Gigabit Ethernet 0/0 (G0/0) | Gigabit Ethernet 0/1 (G0/1) | Serial 0/0/0 (S0/0/0) | Serial 0/0/1 (S0/0/1) |
| **Note**: To find out how the router is configured, look at the interfaces to identify the type of router and how many interfaces the router has. There is no way to effectively list all the combinations of configurations for each router class. This table includes identifiers for the possible combinations of Ethernet and Serial interfaces in the device. The table does not include any other type of interface, even though a specific router may contain one. An example of this might be an ISDN BRI interface. The string in parenthesis is the legal abbreviation that can be used in Cisco IOS commands to represent the interface. | | | | |

# 4.3.1.6 Lab – Troubleshooting Basic Frame Relay

## Topology

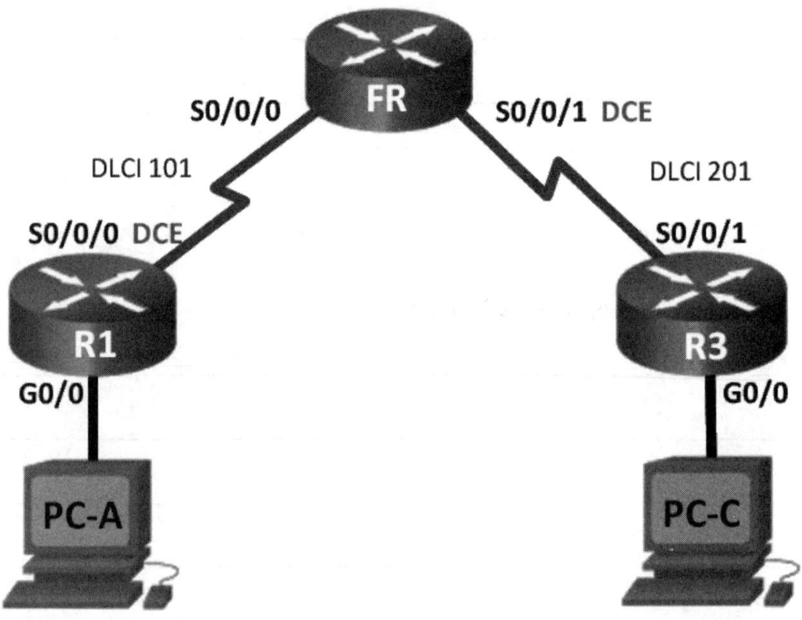


## Addressing Table

| Device | Interface | IP Address | Subnet Mask | Default Gateway |
|---|---|---|---|---|
| R1 | G0/0 | 192.168.1.1 | 255.255.255.0 | N/A |
| | S0/0/0 (DCE) | 10.1.1.1 | 255.255.255.252 | N/A |
| FR | S0/0/0 | N/A | N/A | N/A |
| | S0/0/1 (DCE) | N/A | N/A | N/A |
| R3 | G0/0 | 192.168.3.1 | 255.255.255.0 | N/A |
| | S0/0/1 | 10.1.1.2 | 255.255.255.252 | N/A |
| PC-A | NIC | 192.168.1.3 | 255.255.255.0 | 192.168.1.1 |
| PC-C | NIC | 192.168.3.3 | 255.255.255.0 | 192.168.3.1 |

## Objectives

**Part 1: Build the Network and Load Device Configurations**

**Part 2: Troubleshoot Layer 3 Connectivity**

**Part 3: Troubleshoot Frame Relay**

## Background / Scenario

Frame Relay is a WAN protocol that operates at the physical and data link layers of the OSI reference model. Unlike leased lines, Frame Relay requires only a single-access circuit to the Frame Relay provider to communicate with multiple sites that are connected to the same provider. Configuring Frame Relay at the customer site is generally simple; however, configuration problems can occur.

In this lab, R1 and R3 are experiencing problems communicating with each other. EIGRP is not working and there may also be problems with the Frame Relay configuration. You have been assigned the job of finding and correcting all problems on R1 and R3.

**Note**: The routers used with CCNA hands-on labs are Cisco 1941 Integrated Services Routers (ISRs) with Cisco IOS Release 15.2(4)M3 (universalk9 image). Other routers and Cisco IOS versions can be used. Depending on the model and Cisco IOS version, the commands available and output produced might vary from what is shown in the labs. Refer to the Router Interface Summary Table at the end of this lab for the correct interface identifiers.

**Note**: Make sure that the routers have been erased and have no startup configurations. If you are unsure, contact your instructor.

**Note**: The FR router is acting as the Frame Relay switch, It does NOT have any configuration issues for you to troubleshoot.

## Required Resources

- 3 Routers (Cisco 1941 with Cisco IOS Release 15.2(4)M3 universal image or comparable)
- 2 PCs (Windows 7, Vista, or XP with terminal emulation program, such as Tera Term)
- Console cables to configure the Cisco IOS devices via the console ports
- Ethernet and serial cables as shown in the topology

# Part 1: Build the Network and Load Device Configurations

### Step 1: Cable the network as shown in the topology.

### Step 2: Configure addressing on the PCs.

### Step 3: Load router configuration files.

Load the following configurations into the appropriate router. R1 and R3 have the same passwords. The encrypted privileged EXEC mode password is **class**, and the password for console and vty access is **cisco**.

**Router R1 Configuration:**

```
hostname R1
enable secret class
no ip domain lookup
interface GigabitEthernet0/0
 ip address 192.168.1.1 255.255.255.0

interface Serial0/0/0
 ip address 10.1.1.5 255.255.255.252

 encapsulation frame-relay
 clock rate 128000
 frame-relay map ip 10.1.1.2 101


 no frame-relay inverse-arp
 no shutdown
router eigrp 1
 network 10.1.0.0 0.0.0.3
```

```
 network 192.168.1.0
 eigrp router-id 1.1.1.1
 no auto-summary
line con 0
 password cisco
 logging synchronous
 login
line vty 0 4
 password cisco
 login
end
```

**Router R3 Configuration:**

```
hostname R3
enable secret class
no ip domain lookup
interface GigabitEthernet0/0
 ip address 192.168.30.1 255.255.255.0

no shutdown
interface Serial0/0/1
 ip address 10.1.1.2 255.255.255.252
 encapsulation frame-relay
 frame-relay map ip 10.1.1.2 201
 frame-relay map ip 10.1.1.1 202 broadcast

 no frame-relay inverse-arp
 no shutdown
router eigrp 1
 network 10.1.1.0 0.0.0.3

 eigrp router-id 3.3.3.3
line con 0
 password cisco
 logging synchronous
 login
line vty 0 4
 password cisco
 login
end
```

**Frame Relay Switch (router FR) Configuration:**

```
hostname FR
frame-relay switching
interface Serial0/0/0
 no ip address
```

```
 encapsulation frame-relay
 frame-relay intf-type dce
 frame-relay route 101 interface Serial0/0/1 201
 no shutdown
interface Serial0/0/1
 no ip address
 encapsulation frame-relay
 clock rate 2000000
 frame-relay intf-type dce
 frame-relay route 201 interface Serial0/0/0 101
 no shutdown
end
```

### Step 4: Save your configuration.

## Part 2: Troubleshoot Layer 3 Connectivity

In Part 2, you will verify that Layer 3 connectivity is established on all interfaces. You will need to test IPv4 connectivity for all device interfaces.

### Step 1: Verify that the interfaces listed in the Addressing Table are active and configured with the correct IP address information.

a. Issue the **show ip interface brief** command on R1 and R3 to verify that the interfaces are in an up/up state.

b. Issue the **show run | section interface** command to view all the commands related to interfaces.

c. Resolve all problems found. Record the commands used to correct the configuration.

____________________________________________________________

____________________________________________________________

____________________________________________________________

____________________________________________________________

d. Using **show** commands, verify that R1 and R3 router interfaces match the IP addresses in the Addressing Table.

### Step 2: Verify EIGRP configurations on R1 and R3.

a. Issue the **show ip protocols** command on R1 and R3.

b. Resolve all problems found. Record your answers below.

____________________________________________________________

____________________________________________________________

____________________________________________________________

____________________________________________________________

c. Issue a **show ip route** command on both R1 and R3. Do any EIGRP routes display in the routing table of R1 or R3? ______

## Part 3: Troubleshoot Frame Relay

### Step 1: Test IPv4 end-to-end connectivity.

**Note**: FR (the Frame Relay switch), will NOT have any interfaces for you to ping.

Ping all the active interfaces on R1 and R3. Were the pings successful? Record your ping results in the table below.

| Router | Active Router Interfaces | | | |
|---|---|---|---|---|
| | R1 G0/0 | R1 S0/0/0 | R3 G0/0 | R3 S0/0/1 |
| R1 | | | | |
| R3 | | | | |

Because IPv4 addressing and EIGRP configuration issues have been checked and corrected, the problems must exist with the Frame Relay configuration.

### Step 2: Verify Frame Relay configurations on R1 and R3.

a. Issue the **show frame-relay pvc** command on R1 and R3.

b. Issue the **show frame-relay map** command on R1 and R3.

c. Issue the **show frame-relay lmi** command on R1 and R3.

d. Resolve all problems found. Record your answers below.

______________________________________________

______________________________________________

______________________________________________

______________________________________________

______________________________________________

**Note**: After entering the commands above to fix the Frame Relay problems, communication between the R1, R3, and the Frame Relay switch can take a few minutes before all DLCI communication is resolved.

### Step 3: Verify Frame Relay and EIGRP configurations.

a. Issue a **show ip route eigrp** command on both R1 and R3. Are the LAN networks listed in the output?

_____

b. Issue a **show frame-relay map** command on both R1 and R3. Are the DLCIs active? ________

## Reflection

Describe the troubleshooting methodology you used to solve the issues in this lab. Outline the steps that were necessary to successfully meet the assignment.

_______________________________________________________________________________

## Router Interface Summary Table

| Router Interface Summary | | | | |
|---|---|---|---|---|
| **Router Model** | **Ethernet Interface #1** | **Ethernet Interface #2** | **Serial Interface #1** | **Serial Interface #2** |
| 1800 | Fast Ethernet 0/0 (F0/0) | Fast Ethernet 0/1 (F0/1) | Serial 0/0/0 (S0/0/0) | Serial 0/0/1 (S0/0/1) |
| 1900 | Gigabit Ethernet 0/0 (G0/0) | Gigabit Ethernet 0/1 (G0/1) | Serial 0/0/0 (S0/0/0) | Serial 0/0/1 (S0/0/1) |
| 2801 | Fast Ethernet 0/0 (F0/0) | Fast Ethernet 0/1 (F0/1) | Serial 0/1/0 (S0/1/0) | Serial 0/1/1 (S0/1/1) |
| 2811 | Fast Ethernet 0/0 (F0/0) | Fast Ethernet 0/1 (F0/1) | Serial 0/0/0 (S0/0/0) | Serial 0/0/1 (S0/0/1) |
| 2900 | Gigabit Ethernet 0/0 (G0/0) | Gigabit Ethernet 0/1 (G0/1) | Serial 0/0/0 (S0/0/0) | Serial 0/0/1 (S0/0/1) |

**Note**: To find out how the router is configured, look at the interfaces to identify the type of router and how many interfaces the router has. There is no way to effectively list all the combinations of configurations for each router class. This table includes identifiers for the possible combinations of Ethernet and Serial interfaces in the device. The table does not include any other type of interface, even though a specific router may contain one. An example of this might be an ISDN BRI interface. The string in parenthesis is the legal abbreviation that can be used in Cisco IOS commands to represent the interface.

# 4.4.1.1 Class Activity – Frame Relay Budget Proposal

## Objective

Describe Frame Relay operation.

## Scenario

It has been decided that your company will use Frame Relay technology to provide video connectivity between your main office location and two branch offices. The company will also use the new network for redundancy in case their current ISP network connectivity is interrupted for any reason.

As usual, with any kind of network upgrade, you must develop a cost proposal for your administrator.

After doing some research, you decide to use this Frame Relay web site for your cost analysis. Costs listed on the site are representative of real ISP costs – they are referenced only to help you create your cost analysis design.

For more detailed instructions, open the PDF accompanying this activity.

## Resources

- Packet Tracer software
- Word processing or spreadsheet calculating software

## Directions

### Step 1: Use Packet Tracer to show your home office and two branch offices.

a. Use the Note tool to name the required three routers.

b. Include a Frame Relay router to show where connectivity will be placed on the ISP cloud.

c. Include the ISP cloud in the topology so that the administrators can visualize where the new Frame Relay service will connect to your Frame Relay device or router.

### Step 2: Decide how many DLCI connections you need from your home office to your branch offices.

a. Determine whether to use 1.544 T1 lines for all your DLCI circuits or combination bandwidth connections of varying bandwidths.

b. Be able to justify your decisions made in Step 2a.

### Step 3: Create a Frame Relay cost proposal matrix. Include approximate cost pricing found on the Frame Relay web site. Include in your matrix:

a. Access costs to the ISP

1) Service area tariffs

2) Interstate area tariffs

b. Cost of the Frame Relay ports

c. DLCI costs

### Step 4: Present the cost analysis to solicit comments and approval from the company administrators.

# Chapter 5 — Network Address Translation for IPv4

## 5.0.1.2 Class Activity – Conceptual NAT

### Objective

Describe NAT characteristics.

### Scenario

You work for a large university or school system. Because you are the network administrator, many professors, administrative workers, and other network administrators need your assistance with their networks on a daily basis. They call you at all working hours of the day and, because of the number of telephone calls, you cannot complete your regular network administration tasks.

You need to find a way to limit when you take calls and from whom. You also need to mask your telephone number so that when you call someone, another number is displayed to the recipient.

This scenario describes a very common problem for most small- to medium-sized businesses. Visit, "How Network Address Translation Works" located at http://computer.howstuffworks.com/nat.htm/printable to view more information about how the digital world handles these types of workday interruptions.

Use the PDF provided accompanying this activity to reflect further on how a process, known as NAT, could be the answer to this scenario's challenge.

### Resources

Internet connection

### Directions

#### Step 1: Read Information on the Internet Site.

a. Go to "How Network Address Translation Works" located at http://computer.howstuffworks.com/nat.htm/printable

b. Read the information provided to introduce the basic concepts of NAT.

c. Record five facts you find to be interesting about the NAT process.

#### Step 2: View the NAT graphics.

a. On the same Internet page, look at the types of NAT that are available for configuration on most networks.

b. Define the four NAT types:

1) Static NAT

2) Dynamic NAT

3) NAT Overload

4) NAT Overlap

#### Step 3: Meet together in a full-class setting.

a. Report your five NAT facts to the class.

b. As other students state their interesting facts to the class, check off the stated fact if you already recorded it.

c. If a student reports a fact to the class that you did not record, add it to your list.

# 5.2.2.6 Lab – Configuring Dynamic and Static NAT

## Topology

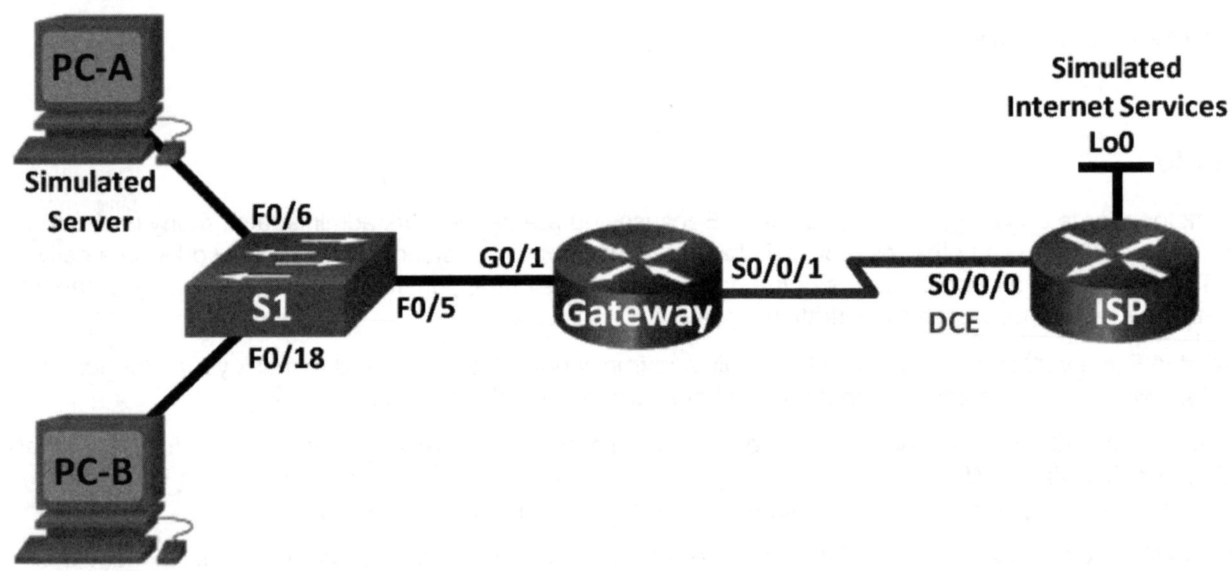


## Addressing Table

| Device | Interface | IP Address | Subnet Mask | Default Gateway |
|---|---|---|---|---|
| Gateway | G0/1 | 192.168.1.1 | 255.255.255.0 | N/A |
| | S0/0/1 | 209.165.201.18 | 255.255.255.252 | N/A |
| ISP | S0/0/0 (DCE) | 209.165.201.17 | 255.255.255.252 | N/A |
| | Lo0 | 192.31.7.1 | 255.255.255.255 | N/A |
| PC-A (Simulated Server) | NIC | 192.168.1.20 | 255.255.255.0 | 192.168.1.1 |
| PC-B | NIC | 192.168.1.21 | 255.255.255.0 | 192.168.1.1 |

## Objectives

**Part 1: Build the Network and Verify Connectivity**

**Part 2: Configure and Verify Static NAT**

**Part 3: Configure and Verify Dynamic NAT**

## Background / Scenario

Network Address Translation (NAT) is the process where a network device, such as a Cisco router, assigns a public address to host devices inside a private network. The main reason to use NAT is to reduce the number of public IP addresses that an organization uses because the number of available IPv4 public addresses is limited.

In this lab, an ISP has allocated the public IP address space of 209.165.200.224/27 to a company. This provides the company with 30 public IP addresses. The addresses, 209.165.200.225 to 209.165.200.241, are for static allocation and 209.165.200.242 to 209.165.200.254 are for dynamic allocation. A static route is used from the ISP to the gateway router, and a default route is used from the gateway to the ISP router. The ISP connection to the Internet is simulated by a loopback address on the ISP router.

**Note**: The routers used with CCNA hands-on labs are Cisco 1941 Integrated Services Routers (ISRs) with Cisco IOS Release 15.2(4)M3 (universalk9 image). The switches used are Cisco Catalyst 2960s with Cisco IOS Release 15.0(2) (lanbasek9 image). Other routers, switches and Cisco IOS versions can be used. Depending on the model and Cisco IOS version, the commands available and output produced might vary from what is shown in the labs. Refer to the Router Interface Summary Table at the end of this lab for the correct interface identifiers.

**Note**: Make sure that the routers and switch have been erased and have no startup configurations. If you are unsure, contact your instructor.

### Required Resources

- 2 Routers (Cisco 1941 with Cisco IOS Release 15.2(4)M3 universal image or comparable)
- 1 Switch (Cisco 2960 with Cisco IOS Release 15.0(2) lanbasek9 image or comparable)
- 2 PCs (Windows 7, Vista, or XP with terminal emulation program, such as Tera Term)
- Console cables to configure the Cisco IOS devices via the console ports
- Ethernet and serial cables as shown in the topology

## Part 1: Build the Network and Verify Connectivity

In Part 1, you will set up the network topology and configure basic settings, such as the interface IP addresses, static routing, device access, and passwords.

### Step 1: Cable the network as shown in the topology.

Attach the devices as shown in the topology diagram, and cable as necessary.

### Step 2: Configure PC hosts.

### Step 3: Initialize and reload the routers and switches as necessary.

### Step 4: Configure basic settings for each router.

a. Disable DNS lookup.

b. Configure IP addresses for the routers as listed in the Addressing Table.

c. Set the clock rate to **128000** for the DCE serial interfaces.

d. Configure device name as shown in the topology.

e. Assign **cisco** as the console and vty passwords.

f. Assign **class** as the encrypted privileged EXEC mode password.

g. Configure **logging synchronous** to prevent console messages from interrupting the command entry.

### Step 5: Create a simulated web server on ISP.

a. Create a local user named **webuser** with an encrypted password of **webpass**.

```
ISP(config)# username webuser privilege 15 secret webpass
```

b. Enable the HTTP server service on ISP.

```
ISP(config)# ip http server
```

c. Configure the HTTP service to use the local user database.

```
ISP(config)# ip http authentication local
```

### Step 6: Configure static routing.

a. Create a static route from the ISP router to the Gateway router using the assigned public network address range 209.165.200.224/27.

```
ISP(config)# ip route 209.165.200.224 255.255.255.224 209.165.201.18
```

b. Create a default route from the Gateway router to the ISP router.

```
Gateway(config)# ip route 0.0.0.0 0.0.0.0 209.165.201.17
```

### Step 7: Save the running configuration to the startup configuration.

### Step 8: Verify network connectivity.

a. From the PC hosts, ping the G0/1 interface on the Gateway router. Troubleshoot if the pings are unsuccessful.

b. Display the routing tables on both routers to verify that the static routes are in the routing table and configured correctly on both routers.

## Part 2: Configure and Verify Static NAT

Static NAT uses a one-to-one mapping of local and global addresses, and these mappings remain constant. Static NAT is particularly useful for web servers or devices that must have static addresses that are accessible from the Internet.

### Step 1: Configure a static mapping.

A static map is configured to tell the router to translate between the private inside server address 192.168.1.20 and the public address 209.165.200.225. This allows a user from the Internet to access PC-A. PC-A is simulating a server or device with a constant address that can be accessed from the Internet.

```
Gateway(config)# ip nat inside source static 192.168.1.20 209.165.200.225
```

### Step 2: Specify the interfaces.

Issue the **ip nat inside** and **ip nat outside** commands to the interfaces.

```
Gateway(config)# interface g0/1
Gateway(config-if)# ip nat inside
Gateway(config-if)# interface s0/0/1
Gateway(config-if)# ip nat outside
```

### Step 3: Test the configuration.

a. Display the static NAT table by issuing the **show ip nat translations** command.

```
Gateway# show ip nat translations
```

```
Pro Inside global        Inside local       Outside local      Outside global
--- 209.165.200.225      192.168.1.20       ---                ---
```

What is the translation of the Inside local host address?

192.168.1.20 = ______________________________

The Inside global address is assigned by?

______________________________

The Inside local address is assigned by?

______________________________

b. From PC-A, ping the Lo0 interface (192.31.7.1) on ISP. If the ping was unsuccessful, troubleshoot and correct the issues. On the Gateway router, display the NAT table.

```
Gateway# show ip nat translations
Pro Inside global         Inside local       Outside local      Outside global
icmp 209.165.200.225:1 192.168.1.20:1       192.31.7.1:1       192.31.7.1:1
--- 209.165.200.225      192.168.1.20       ---                ---
```

A NAT entry was added to the table with ICMP listed as the protocol when PC-A sent an ICMP request (ping) to 192.31.7.1 on ISP.

What port number was used in this ICMP exchange? ____________

**Note**: It may be necessary to disable the PC-A firewall for the ping to be successful.

c. From PC-A, telnet to the ISP Lo0 interface and display the NAT table.

```
Pro Inside global            Inside local         Outside local      Outside global
icmp 209.165.200.225:1      192.168.1.20:1       192.31.7.1:1       192.31.7.1:1
tcp 209.165.200.225:1034 192.168.1.20:1034    192.31.7.1:23      192.31.7.1:23
--- 209.165.200.225         192.168.1.20         ---                ---
```

**Note**: The NAT for the ICMP request may have timed out and been removed from the NAT table.

What was the protocol used in this translation? __________

What are the port numbers used?

Inside global / local: ____________

Outside global / local: ____________

d. Because static NAT was configured for PC-A, verify that pinging from ISP to PC-A at the static NAT public address (209.165.200.225) is successful.

e. On the Gateway router, display the NAT table to verify the translation.

```
Gateway# show ip nat translations
Pro Inside global          Inside local        Outside local        Outside global
icmp 209.165.200.225:12 192.168.1.20:12      209.165.201.17:12   209.165.201.17:12
--- 209.165.200.225       192.168.1.20        ---                  ---
```

Notice that the Outside local and Outside global addresses are the same. This address is the ISP remote network source address. For the ping from the ISP to succeed, the Inside global static NAT address 209.165.200.225 was translated to the Inside local address of PC-A (192.168.1.20).

f. Verify NAT statistics by using the **show ip nat statistics** command on the Gateway router.

```
Gateway# show ip nat statistics
Total active translations: 2 (1 static, 1 dynamic; 1 extended)
Peak translations: 2, occurred 00:02:12 ago
Outside interfaces:
  Serial0/0/1
Inside interfaces:
  GigabitEthernet0/1
Hits: 39  Misses: 0
CEF Translated packets: 39, CEF Punted packets: 0
Expired translations: 3
Dynamic mappings:

Total doors: 0
Appl doors: 0
Normal doors: 0
Queued Packets: 0
```

**Note**: This is only a sample output. Your output may not match exactly.

## Part 3: Configure and Verify Dynamic NAT

Dynamic NAT uses a pool of public addresses and assigns them on a first-come, first-served basis. When an inside device requests access to an outside network, dynamic NAT assigns an available public IPv4 address from the pool. Dynamic NAT results in a many-to-many address mapping between local and global addresses.

### Step 1: Clear NATs.

Before proceeding to add dynamic NATs, clear the NATs and statistics from Part 2.

```
Gateway# clear ip nat translation *
Gateway# clear ip nat statistics
```

### Step 2: Define an access control list (ACL) that matches the LAN private IP address range.

ACL 1 is used to allow 192.168.1.0/24 network to be translated.

```
Gateway(config)# access-list 1 permit 192.168.1.0 0.0.0.255
```

### Step 3: Verify that the NAT interface configurations are still valid.

Issue the **show ip nat statistics** command on the Gateway router to verify the NAT configurations.

### Step 4: Define the pool of usable public IP addresses.

```
Gateway(config)# ip nat pool public_access 209.165.200.242 209.165.200.254 net-
mask 255.255.255.224
```

### Step 5: Define the NAT from the inside source list to the outside pool.

**Note**: Remember that NAT pool names are case-sensitive and the pool name entered here must match that used in the previous step.

```
Gateway(config)# ip nat inside source list 1 pool public_access
```

### Step 6: Test the configuration.

a. From PC-B, ping the Lo0 interface (192.31.7.1) on ISP. If the ping was unsuccessful, troubleshoot and correct the issues. On the Gateway router, display the NAT table.

```
Gateway# show ip nat translations
Pro Inside global        Inside local      Outside local      Outside global
--- 209.165.200.225      192.168.1.20      ---                ---
icmp 209.165.200.242:1 192.168.1.21:1      192.31.7.1:1       192.31.7.1:1
--- 209.165.200.242      192.168.1.21      ---                ---
```

What is the translation of the Inside local host address for PC-B?

192.168.1.21 = ____________________

A dynamic NAT entry was added to the table with ICMP as the protocol when PC-B sent an ICMP message to 192.31.7.1 on ISP.

What port number was used in this ICMP exchange? __________

b. From PC-B, open a browser and enter the IP address of the ISP-simulated web server (Lo0 interface). When prompted, log in as **webuser** with a password of **webpass**.

c. Display the NAT table.

```
Pro Inside global          Inside local         Outside local      Outside global
--- 209.165.200.225        192.168.1.20         ---                ---
tcp 209.165.200.242:1038 192.168.1.21:1038 192.31.7.1:80      192.31.7.1:80
tcp 209.165.200.242:1039 192.168.1.21:1039 192.31.7.1:80      192.31.7.1:80
tcp 209.165.200.242:1040 192.168.1.21:1040 192.31.7.1:80      192.31.7.1:80
tcp 209.165.200.242:1041 192.168.1.21:1041 192.31.7.1:80      192.31.7.1:80
tcp 209.165.200.242:1042 192.168.1.21:1042 192.31.7.1:80      192.31.7.1:80
tcp 209.165.200.242:1043 192.168.1.21:1043 192.31.7.1:80      192.31.7.1:80
tcp 209.165.200.242:1044 192.168.1.21:1044 192.31.7.1:80      192.31.7.1:80
tcp 209.165.200.242:1045 192.168.1.21:1045 192.31.7.1:80      192.31.7.1:80
tcp 209.165.200.242:1046 192.168.1.21:1046 192.31.7.1:80      192.31.7.1:80
tcp 209.165.200.242:1047 192.168.1.21:1047 192.31.7.1:80      192.31.7.1:80
tcp 209.165.200.242:1048 192.168.1.21:1048 192.31.7.1:80      192.31.7.1:80
tcp 209.165.200.242:1049 192.168.1.21:1049 192.31.7.1:80      192.31.7.1:80
tcp 209.165.200.242:1050 192.168.1.21:1050 192.31.7.1:80      192.31.7.1:80
tcp 209.165.200.242:1051 192.168.1.21:1051 192.31.7.1:80      192.31.7.1:80
tcp 209.165.200.242:1052 192.168.1.21:1052 192.31.7.1:80      192.31.7.1:80
--- 209.165.200.242      192.168.1.22         ---                ---
```

What protocol was used in this translation? __________

What port numbers were used?

Inside: ________________

outside: ________________

What well-known port number and service was used? ________________

d. Verify NAT statistics by using the **show ip nat statistics** command on the Gateway router.

```
Gateway# show ip nat statistics
Total active translations: 3 (1 static, 2 dynamic; 1 extended)
Peak translations: 17, occurred 00:06:40 ago
Outside interfaces:
  Serial0/0/1
Inside interfaces:
  GigabitEthernet0/1
Hits: 345  Misses: 0
CEF Translated packets: 345, CEF Punted packets: 0
Expired translations: 20
Dynamic mappings:
-- Inside Source
[Id: 1] access-list 1 pool public_access refcount 2
 pool public_access: netmask 255.255.255.224
        start 209.165.200.242 end 209.165.200.254
        type generic, total addresses 13, allocated 1 (7%), misses 0

Total doors: 0
Appl doors: 0
Normal doors: 0
Queued Packets: 0
```

**Note**: This is only a sample output. Your output may not match exactly.

### Step 7: Remove the static NAT entry.

In Step 7, the static NAT entry is removed and you can observe the NAT entry.

a. Remove the static NAT from Part 2. Enter **yes** when prompted to delete child entries.

```
Gateway(config)# no ip nat inside source static 192.168.1.20 209.165.200.225

Static entry in use, do you want to delete child entries? [no]: yes
```

b. Clear the NATs and statistics.

c. Ping the ISP (192.31.7.1) from both hosts.

d. Display the NAT table and statistics.

```
Gateway# show ip nat statistics
Total active translations: 4 (0 static, 4 dynamic; 2 extended)
Peak translations: 15, occurred 00:00:43 ago
Outside interfaces:
  Serial0/0/1
Inside interfaces:
  GigabitEthernet0/1
Hits: 16  Misses: 0
CEF Translated packets: 285, CEF Punted packets: 0
Expired translations: 11
```

```
Dynamic mappings:
-- Inside Source
[Id: 1] access-list 1 pool public_access refcount 4
 pool public_access: netmask 255.255.255.224
        start 209.165.200.242 end 209.165.200.254
        type generic, total addresses 13, allocated 2 (15%), misses 0

Total doors: 0
Appl doors: 0
Normal doors: 0
Queued Packets: 0

Gateway# show ip nat translation
Pro Inside global       Inside local        Outside local       Outside global
icmp 209.165.200.243:512 192.168.1.20:512 192.31.7.1:512      192.31.7.1:512
--- 209.165.200.243     192.168.1.20        ---                 ---
icmp 209.165.200.242:512 192.168.1.21:512 192.31.7.1:512      192.31.7.1:512
--- 209.165.200.242     192.168.1.21        ---                 ---
```

**Note**: This is only a sample output. Your output may not match exactly.

## Reflection

1. Why would NAT be used in a network?

_______________________________________________

_______________________________________________

_______________________________________________

2. What are the limitations of NAT?

_______________________________________________

_______________________________________________

_______________________________________________

## Router Interface Summary Table

| Router Interface Summary | | | | |
|---|---|---|---|---|
| **Router Model** | **Ethernet Interface #1** | **Ethernet Interface #2** | **Serial Interface #1** | **Serial Interface #2** |
| 1800 | Fast Ethernet 0/0 (F0/0) | Fast Ethernet 0/1 (F0/1) | Serial 0/0/0 (S0/0/0) | Serial 0/0/1 (S0/0/1) |
| 1900 | Gigabit Ethernet 0/0 (G0/0) | Gigabit Ethernet 0/1 (G0/1) | Serial 0/0/0 (S0/0/0) | Serial 0/0/1 (S0/0/1) |
| 2801 | Fast Ethernet 0/0 (F0/0) | Fast Ethernet 0/1 (F0/1) | Serial 0/1/0 (S0/1/0) | Serial 0/1/1 (S0/1/1) |
| 2811 | Fast Ethernet 0/0 (F0/0) | Fast Ethernet 0/1 (F0/1) | Serial 0/0/0 (S0/0/0) | Serial 0/0/1 (S0/0/1) |
| 2900 | Gigabit Ethernet 0/0 (G0/0) | Gigabit Ethernet 0/1 (G0/1) | Serial 0/0/0 (S0/0/0) | Serial 0/0/1 (S0/0/1) |
| **Note**: To find out how the router is configured, look at the interfaces to identify the type of router and how many interfaces the router has. There is no way to effectively list all the combinations of configurations for each router class. This table includes identifiers for the possible combinations of Ethernet and Serial interfaces in the device. The table does not include any other type of interface, even though a specific router may contain one. An example of this might be an ISDN BRI interface. The string in parenthesis is the legal abbreviation that can be used in Cisco IOS commands to represent the interface. | | | | |

# 5.2.3.7 Lab – Configuring Port Address Translation (PAT)

## Topology

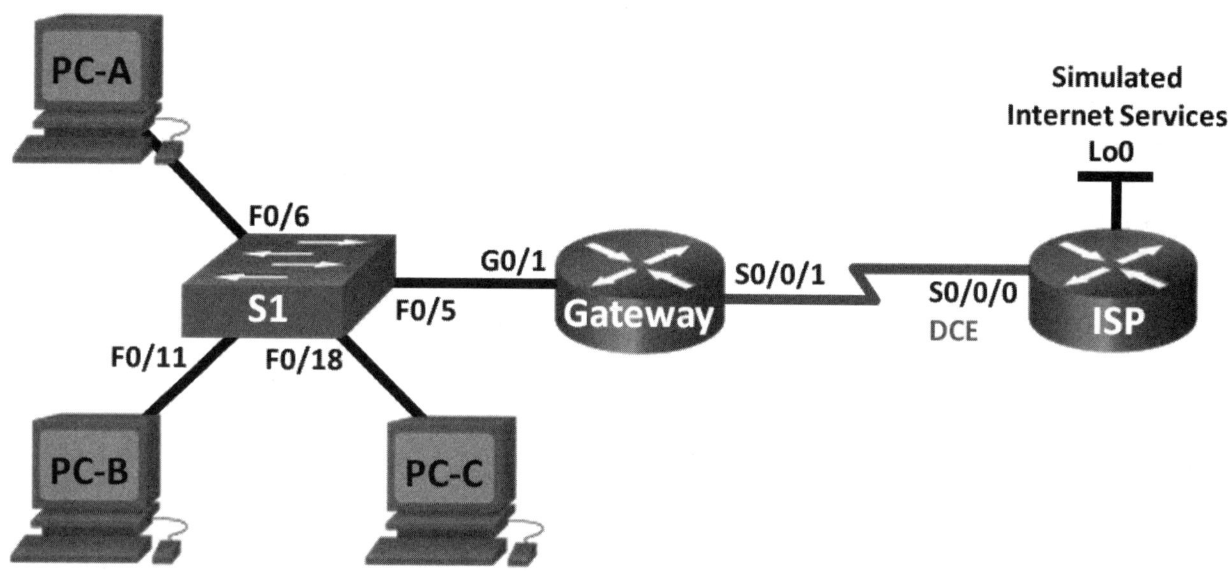


## Addressing Table

| Device | Interface | IP Address | Subnet Mask | Default Gateway |
|---|---|---|---|---|
| Gateway | G0/1 | 192.168.1.1 | 255.255.255.0 | N/A |
| | S0/0/1 | 209.165.201.18 | 255.255.255.252 | N/A |
| ISP | S0/0/0 (DCE) | 209.165.201.17 | 255.255.255.252 | N/A |
| | Lo0 | 192.31.7.1 | 255.255.255.255 | N/A |
| PC-A | NIC | 192.168.1.20 | 255.255.255.0 | 192.168.1.1 |
| PC-B | NIC | 192.168.1.21 | 255.255.255.0 | 192.168.1.1 |
| PC-C | NIC | 192.168.1.22 | 255.255.255.0 | 192.168.1.1 |

## Objectives

**Part 1: Build the Network and Verify Connectivity**

**Part 2: Configure and Verify NAT Pool Overload**

**Part 3: Configure and Verify PAT**

## Background / Scenario

In the first part of the lab, your company is allocated the public IP address range of 209.165.200.224/29 by the ISP. This provides the company with six public IP addresses. Dynamic NAT pool overload uses a pool of IP addresses in a many-to-many relationship. The router uses the first IP address in the pool and assigns connections using the IP address plus a unique port number. After the maximum number of translations for a single IP address have been reached on the router (platform and hardware specific), it uses the next IP address in the pool. NAT pool overload is a form port address translation (PAT) that overloads a group of public IPv4 addresses.

In Part 2, the ISP has allocated a single IP address, 209.165.201.18, to your company for use on the Internet connection from the company Gateway router to the ISP. You will use the PAT to convert multiple internal addresses into the one usable public address. You will test, view, and verify that the translations are taking place, and you will interpret the NAT/PAT statistics to monitor the process.

**Note**: The routers used with CCNA hands-on labs are Cisco 1941 Integrated Services Routers (ISRs) with Cisco IOS Release 15.2(4)M3 (universalk9 image). The switches used are Cisco Catalyst 2960s with Cisco IOS Release 15.0(2) (lanbasek9 image). Other routers, switches and Cisco IOS versions can be used. Depending on the model and Cisco IOS version, the commands available and output produced might vary from what is shown in the labs. Refer to the Router Interface Summary Table at the end of this lab for the correct interface identifiers.

**Note**: Make sure that the routers and switch have been erased and have no startup configurations. If you are unsure, contact your instructor.

### Required Resources

- 2 Routers (Cisco 1941 with Cisco IOS Release 15.2(4)M3 universal image or comparable)
- 1 Switch (Cisco 2960 with Cisco IOS Release 15.0(2) lanbasek9 image or comparable)
- 3 PCs (Windows 7, Vista, or XP with terminal emulation program, such as Tera Term)
- Console cables to configure the Cisco IOS devices via the console ports
- Ethernet and serial cables as shown in the topology

## Part 1: Build the Network and Verify Connectivity

In Part 1, you will set up the network topology and configure basic settings, such as the interface IP addresses, static routing, device access, and passwords.

### Step 1: Cable the network as shown in the topology.

### Step 2: Configure PC hosts.

### Step 3: Initialize and reload the routers and switches.

### Step 4: Configure basic settings for each router.

a. Disable DNS lookup.

b. Configure IP addresses for the routers as listed in the Addressing Table.

c. Set the clock rate to **128000** for DCE serial interface.

d. Configure device name as shown in the topology.

e. Assign **cisco** as the console and vty passwords.

f. Assign **class** as the encrypted privileged EXEC mode password.

g. Configure **logging synchronous** to prevent console messages from interrupting the command entry.

### Step 5: Configure static routing.

a. Create a static route from the ISP router to the Gateway router.

```
ISP(config)# ip route 209.165.200.224 255.255.255.248 209.165.201.18
```

b. Create a default route from the Gateway router to the ISP router.

```
Gateway(config)# ip route 0.0.0.0 0.0.0.0 209.165.201.17
```

### Step 6: Verify network connectivity.

a. From the PC hosts, ping the G0/1 interface on the Gateway router. Troubleshoot if the pings are unsuccessful.

b. Verify that the static routes are configured correctly on both routers.

## Part 2: Configure and Verify NAT Pool Overload

In Part 2, you will configure the Gateway router to translate the IP addresses from the 192.168.1.0/24 network to one of the six usable addresses in the 209.165.200.224/29 range.

### Step 1: Define an access control list that matches the LAN private IP addresses.

ACL 1 is used to allow the 192.168.1.0/24 network to be translated.

```
Gateway(config)# access-list 1 permit 192.168.1.0 0.0.0.255
```

### Step 2: Define the pool of usable public IP addresses.

```
Gateway(config)# ip nat pool public_access 209.165.200.225  209.165.200.230
netmask 255.255.255.248
```

### Step 3: Define the NAT from the inside source list to the outside pool.

```
Gateway(config)# ip nat inside source list 1 pool public_access overload
```

### Step 4: Specify the interfaces.

Issue the **ip nat inside** and **ip nat outside** commands to the interfaces.

```
Gateway(config)# interface g0/1
Gateway(config-if)# ip nat inside
Gateway(config-if)# interface s0/0/1
Gateway(config-if)# ip nat outside
```

### Step 5: Verify the NAT pool overload configuration.

a. From each PC host, ping the 192.31.7.1 address on the ISP router.

b. Display NAT statistics on the Gateway router.

```
Gateway# show ip nat statistics
Total active translations: 3 (0 static, 3 dynamic; 3 extended)
Peak translations: 3, occurred 00:00:25 ago
Outside interfaces:
  Serial0/0/1
Inside interfaces:
  GigabitEthernet0/1
Hits: 24  Misses: 0
```

```
CEF Translated packets: 24, CEF Punted packets: 0
Expired translations: 0
Dynamic mappings:
-- Inside Source
[Id: 1] access-list 1 pool public_access refcount 3
 pool public_access: netmask 255.255.255.248
        start 209.165.200.225 end 209.165.200.230
        type generic, total addresses 6, allocated 1 (16%), misses 0

Total doors: 0
Appl doors: 0
Normal doors: 0
Queued Packets: 0
```

c. Display NATs on the Gateway router.

```
Gateway# show ip nat translations
Pro Inside global         Inside local        Outside local      Outside global
icmp 209.165.200.225:0 192.168.1.20:1      192.31.7.1:1       192.31.7.1:0
icmp 209.165.200.225:1 192.168.1.21:1      192.31.7.1:1       192.31.7.1:1
icmp 209.165.200.225:2 192.168.1.22:1      192.31.7.1:1       192.31.7.1:2
```

**Note**: Depending on how much time has elapsed since you performed the pings from each PC, you may not see all three translations. ICMP translations have a short timeout value.

How many Inside local IP addresses are listed in the sample output above? __________

How many Inside global IP addresses are listed? __________

How many port numbers are used paired with the Inside global addresses? __________

What would be the result of pinging the Inside local address of PC-A from the ISP router? Why?

______________________________________________________________________

______________________________________________________________________

## Part 3: Configure and Verify PAT

In Part 3, you will configure PAT by using an interface instead of a pool of addresses to define the outside address. Not all of the commands in Part 2 will be reused in Part 3.

### Step 1: Clear NATs and statistics on the Gateway router.

### Step 2: Verify the configuration for NAT.

a. Verify that statistics have been cleared.

b. Verify that the outside and inside interfaces are configured for NATs.

c. Verify that the ACL is still configured for NATs.

What command did you use to confirm the results from steps a to c?

______________________________________________________________________

### Step 3: Remove the pool of useable public IP addresses.

```
Gateway(config)# no ip nat pool public_access 209.165.200.225 209.165.200.230
netmask 255.255.255.248
```

### Step 4: Remove the NAT translation from inside source list to outside pool.

```
Gateway(config)# no ip nat inside source list 1 pool public_access overload
```

### Step 5: Associate the source list with the outside interface.

```
Gateway(config)# ip nat inside source list 1 interface serial 0/0/1 overload
```

### Step 6: Test the PAT configuration.

a. From each PC, ping the 192.31.7.1 address on the ISP router.

b. Display NAT statistics on the Gateway router.

```
Gateway# show ip nat statistics
Total active translations: 3 (0 static, 3 dynamic; 3 extended)
Peak translations: 3, occurred 00:00:19 ago
Outside interfaces:
  Serial0/0/1
Inside interfaces:
  GigabitEthernet0/1
Hits: 24  Misses: 0
CEF Translated packets: 24, CEF Punted packets: 0
Expired translations: 0
Dynamic mappings:
-- Inside Source
[Id: 2] access-list 1 interface Serial0/0/1 refcount 3

Total doors: 0
Appl doors: 0
Normal doors: 0
Queued Packets: 0
```

c. Display NAT translations on Gateway.

```
Gateway# show ip nat translations
Pro Inside global        Inside local       Outside local      Outside global
icmp 209.165.201.18:3   192.168.1.20:1     192.31.7.1:1       192.31.7.1:3
icmp 209.165.201.18:1   192.168.1.21:1     192.31.7.1:1       192.31.7.1:1
icmp 209.165.201.18:4   192.168.1.22:1     192.31.7.1:1       192.31.7.1:4
```

## Reflection

What advantages does PAT provide?

_______________________________________________________________________________

## Router Interface Summary Table

| Router Interface Summary | | | | |
|---|---|---|---|---|
| **Router Model** | **Ethernet Interface #1** | **Ethernet Interface #2** | **Serial Interface #1** | **Serial Interface #2** |
| 1800 | Fast Ethernet 0/0 (F0/0) | Fast Ethernet 0/1 (F0/1) | Serial 0/0/0 (S0/0/0) | Serial 0/0/1 (S0/0/1) |
| 1900 | Gigabit Ethernet 0/0 (G0/0) | Gigabit Ethernet 0/1 (G0/1) | Serial 0/0/0 (S0/0/0) | Serial 0/0/1 (S0/0/1) |
| 2801 | Fast Ethernet 0/0 (F0/0) | Fast Ethernet 0/1 (F0/1) | Serial 0/1/0 (S0/1/0) | Serial 0/1/1 (S0/1/1) |
| 2811 | Fast Ethernet 0/0 (F0/0) | Fast Ethernet 0/1 (F0/1) | Serial 0/0/0 (S0/0/0) | Serial 0/0/1 (S0/0/1) |
| 2900 | Gigabit Ethernet 0/0 (G0/0) | Gigabit Ethernet 0/1 (G0/1) | Serial 0/0/0 (S0/0/0) | Serial 0/0/1 (S0/0/1) |
| **Note**: To find out how the router is configured, look at the interfaces to identify the type of router and how many interfaces the router has. There is no way to effectively list all the combinations of configurations for each router class. This table includes identifiers for the possible combinations of Ethernet and Serial interfaces in the device. The table does not include any other type of interface, even though a specific router may contain one. An example of this might be an ISDN BRI interface. The string in parenthesis is the legal abbreviation that can be used in Cisco IOS commands to represent the interface. | | | | |

# 5.3.1.5 Lab – Troubleshooting NAT Configurations

## Topology

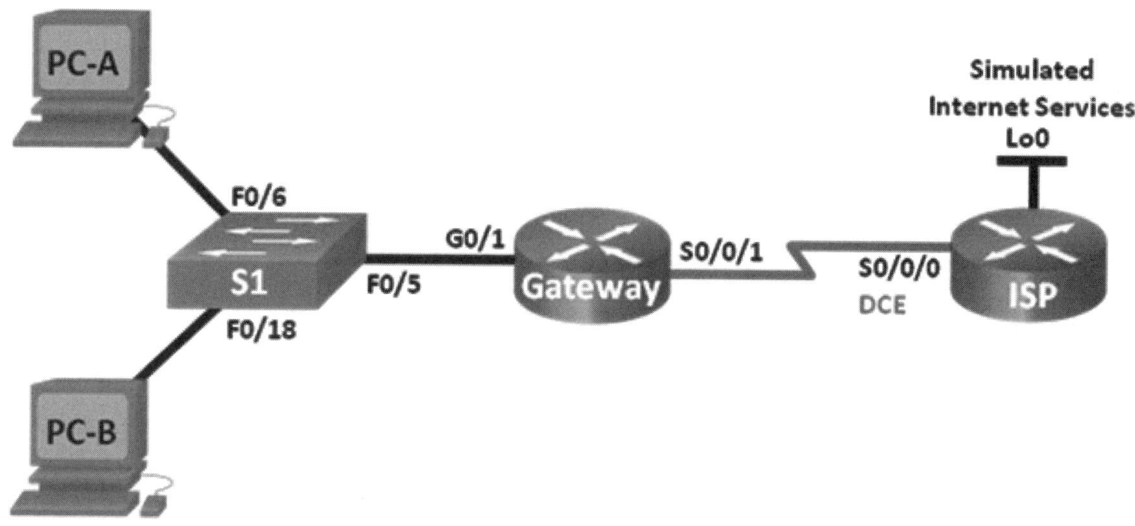


## Addressing Table

| Device | Interface | IP Address | Subnet Mask | Default Gateway |
|---|---|---|---|---|
| Gateway | G0/1 | 192.168.1.1 | 255.255.255.0 | N/A |
| | S0/0/1 | 209.165.200.225 | 255.255.255.252 | N/A |
| ISP | S0/0/0 (DCE) | 209.165.200.226 | 255.255.255.252 | N/A |
| | Lo0 | 198.133.219.1 | 255.255.255.255 | N/A |
| PC-A | NIC | 192.168.1.3 | 255.255.255.0 | 192.168.1.1 |
| PC-B | NIC | 192.168.1.4 | 255.255.255.0 | 192.168.1.1 |

## Objectives

**Part 1: Build the Network and Configure Basic Device Settings**

**Part 2: Troubleshoot Static NAT**

**Part 3: Troubleshoot Dynamic NAT**

## Background / Scenario

In this lab, the Gateway router was configured by an inexperienced network administrator at your company. Several errors in the configuration have resulted in NAT issues. Your boss has asked you to troubleshoot and correct the NAT errors and document your work. Ensure that the network supports the following:

- PC-A acts as a web server with a static NAT and will be reachable from the outside using the 209.165.200.254 address.
- PC-B acts as a host computer and dynamically receives an IP address from the created pool of addresses called NAT_POOL, which uses the 209.165.200.240/29 range.

**Note**: The routers used with CCNA hands-on labs are Cisco 1941 Integrated Services Routers (ISRs) with Cisco IOS Release 15.2(4)M3 (universalk9 image). The switches used are Cisco Catalyst 2960s with Cisco IOS Release 15.0(2) (lanbasek9 image). Other routers, switches and Cisco IOS versions can be used. Depending on the model and Cisco IOS version, the commands available and output produced might vary from what is shown in the labs. Refer to the Router Interface Summary Table at the end of this lab for the correct interface identifiers.

**Note**: Make sure that the routers and switch have been erased and have no startup configurations. If you are unsure, contact your instructor.

### Required Resources

- 2 Routers (Cisco 1941 with Cisco IOS Release 15.2(4)M3 universal image or comparable)
- 1 Switch (Cisco 2960 with Cisco IOS Release 15.0(2) lanbasek9 image or comparable)
- 2 PCs (Windows 7, Vista, or XP with terminal emulation program, such as Tera Term)
- Console cables to configure the Cisco IOS devices via the console ports
- Ethernet and serial cables as shown in the topology

## Part 1: Build the Network and Configure Basic Device Settings

In Part 1, you will set up the network topology and configure the routers with basic settings. Additional NAT-related configurations are provided. The NAT configurations for the Gateway router contains errors that you will identify and correct as you proceed through the lab.

### Step 1: Cable the network as shown in the topology.

### Step 2: Configure PC hosts.

### Step 3: Initialize and reload the switch and routers.

### Step 4: Configure basic settings for each router.

a. Disable DNS lookup.

b. Configure device name as shown in the topology.

c. Configure IP addresses as listed in the Address Table.

d. Set the clock rate to **128000** for DCE serial interfaces.

e. Assign **cisco** as the console and vty password.

f. Assign **class** as the encrypted privileged EXEC mode password.

g. Configure **logging synchronous** to prevent console messages from interrupting the command entry.

### Step 5: Configure static routing.

a. Create a static route from the ISP router to the Gateway router-assigned public network address range 209.165.200.224/27.

```
ISP(config)# ip route 209.165.200.224 255.255.255.224 s0/0/0
```

b. Create a default route from the Gateway router to the ISP router.

```
Gateway(config)# ip route 0.0.0.0 0.0.0.0 s0/0/1
```

### Step 6: Load router configurations.

The configurations for the routers are provided for you. There are errors with the configuration for the Gateway router. Identify and correct the configurations errors.

#### Gateway Router Configuration

```
interface g0/1
 ip nat outside

 no shutdown
interface s0/0/0
 ip nat outside

interface s0/0/1

 no shutdown
ip nat inside source static 192.168.2.3 209.165.200.254

ip nat pool NAT_POOL 209.165.200.241 209.165.200.246 netmask 255.255.255.248
ip nat inside source list NAT_ACL pool NATPOOL

ip access-list standard NAT_ACL
 permit 192.168.10.0 0.0.0.255

banner motd $AUTHORIZED ACCESS ONLY$
end
```

### Step 7: Save the running configuration to the startup configuration.

## Part 2: Troubleshoot Static NAT

In Part 2, you will examine the static NAT for PC-A to determine if it is configured correctly. You will troubleshoot the scenario until the correct static NAT is verified.

a. To troubleshoot issues with NAT, use the **debug ip nat** command. Turn on NAT debugging to see translations in real-time across the Gateway router.

```
Gateway# debug ip nat
```

b. From PC-A, ping Lo0 on the ISP router. Do any NAT debug translations appear on the Gateway router?

____________________________________________________________________________

c. On the Gateway router, enter the command that allows you to see all current NAT translations on the Gateway router. Write the command in the space below.

____________________________________________________________________________

Why are you seeing a NAT translation in the table, but none occurred when PC-A pinged the ISP loopback interface? What is needed to correct the issue?

____________________________________________________________________________

d. Record any commands that are necessary to correct the static NAT configuration error.

____________________________________________

____________________________________________

e. From PC-A, ping Lo0 on the ISP router. Do any NAT debug translations appear on the Gateway router?

____________________________________________

f. On the Gateway router, enter the command that allows you to observe the total number of current NATs. Write the command in the space below.

____________________________________________

Is the static NAT occurring successfully? Why?

____________________________________________

g. On the Gateway router, enter the command that allows you to view the current configuration of the router. Write the command in the space below.

____________________________________________

h. Are there any problems with the current configuration that prevent the static NAT from occurring?

____________________________________________

i. Record any commands that are necessary to correct the static NAT configuration errors.

____________________________________________

____________________________________________

____________________________________________

j. From PC-A, ping Lo0 on the ISP router. Do any NAT debug translations appear on the Gateway router?

____________________________________________

k. Use the **show ip nat translations verbose** command to verify static NAT functionality.

**Note**: The timeout value for ICMP is very short. If you do not see all the translations in the output, redo the ping.

Is the static NAT translation occurring successfully? ____________________

If static NAT is not occurring, repeat the steps above to troubleshoot the configuration.

## Part 3: Troubleshoot Dynamic NAT

a. From PC-B, ping Lo0 on the ISP router. Do any NAT debug translations appear on the Gateway router?

________________

b. On the Gateway router, enter the command that allows you to view the current configuration of the router. Are there any problems with the current configuration that prevent dynamic NAT from occurring?

____________________________________________

c. Record any commands that are necessary to correct the dynamic NAT configuration errors.

____________________________________________

____________________________________________

____________________________________________

d. From PC-B, ping Lo0 on the ISP router. Do any NAT debug translations appear on the Gateway router?

____________________________________________

e. Use the **show ip nat statistics** to view NAT usage.

Is the NAT occurring successfully? ____________

What percentage of dynamic addresses has been allocated? ________

f. Turn off all debugging using the **undebug all** command.

## Reflection

1. What is the benefit of a static NAT?

____________________________________________

____________________________________________

2. What issues would arise if 10 host computers in this network were attempting simultaneous Internet communication?

____________________________________________

____________________________________________

## Router Interface Summary Table

| Router Interface Summary | | | | |
|---|---|---|---|---|
| **Router Model** | **Ethernet Interface #1** | **Ethernet Interface #2** | **Serial Interface #1** | **Serial Interface #2** |
| 1800 | Fast Ethernet 0/0 (F0/0) | Fast Ethernet 0/1 (F0/1) | Serial 0/0/0 (S0/0/0) | Serial 0/0/1 (S0/0/1) |
| 1900 | Gigabit Ethernet 0/0 (G0/0) | Gigabit Ethernet 0/1 (G0/1) | Serial 0/0/0 (S0/0/0) | Serial 0/0/1 (S0/0/1) |
| 2801 | Fast Ethernet 0/0 (F0/0) | Fast Ethernet 0/1 (F0/1) | Serial 0/1/0 (S0/1/0) | Serial 0/1/1 (S0/1/1) |
| 2811 | Fast Ethernet 0/0 (F0/0) | Fast Ethernet 0/1 (F0/1) | Serial 0/0/0 (S0/0/0) | Serial 0/0/1 (S0/0/1) |
| 2900 | Gigabit Ethernet 0/0 (G0/0) | Gigabit Ethernet 0/1 (G0/1) | Serial 0/0/0 (S0/0/0) | Serial 0/0/1 (S0/0/1) |

**Note**: To find out how the router is configured, look at the interfaces to identify the type of router and how many interfaces the router has. There is no way to effectively list all the combinations of configurations for each router class. This table includes identifiers for the possible combinations of Ethernet and Serial interfaces in the device. The table does not include any other type of interface, even though a specific router may contain one. An example of this might be an ISDN BRI interface. The string in parenthesis is the legal abbreviation that can be used in Cisco IOS commands to represent the interface.

# 5.4.1.1 Class Activity – NAT Check

## Objective

Configure, verify and analyze static NAT, dynamic NAT and NAT with overloading.

## Scenario

Network address translation is not currently included in your company's network design. It has been decided to configure some devices to use NAT services for connecting to the mail server.

Before deploying NAT live on the network, you prototype it using a network simulation program.

## Resources

- Packet Tracer software
- Word processing or presentation software

## Directions

### Step 1: Create a very small network topology using Packet Tracer, including, at minimum:

a. Two 1941 routers, interconnected

b. Two LAN switches, one per router

c. One mail server, connected to the LAN on one router

d. One PC or laptop, connected the LAN on the other router

### Step 2: Address the topology.

a. Use private addressing for all networks, hosts, and device.

b. DHCP addressing of the PC or laptop is optional.

c. Static addressing of the mail server is mandatory.

### Step 3: Configure a routing protocol for the network.

### Step 4: Validate full network connectivity without NAT services.

a. Ping from one end of the topology and back to ensure the network is functioning fully.

b. Troubleshoot and correct any problems preventing full network functionality.

### Step 5: Configure NAT services on either router from the host PC or laptop to the mail server

### Step 6: Produce output validating NAT operations on the simulated network.

a. Use the **show ip nat statistics**, **show access-lists**, and **show ip nat translations** commands to gather information about NAT's operation on the router

b. Copy and paste or save screenshots of the topology and output information to a word processing or presentation document.

### Step 7: Explain the NAT design and output to another group or to the class.

# Chapter 6 — Broadband Solutions

## 6.0.1.2 Class Activity – Broadband Varieties

### Objective

Select broadband solutions to support remote connectivity in a small- to medium-sized business network.

### Scenario

Telework employment opportunities are expanding in your local area every day. You have been offered employment as a teleworker for a major corporation. The new employer requires teleworkers to have access the Internet to fulfill their job responsibilities.

Research the following broadband Internet connection types that are available in your geographic area:

- DSL
- Cable
- Satellite

Consider the advantages and disadvantages of each broadband variation as you notate your research, which may include cost, speed, security, and ease of implementation or installation.

### Resources

- World Wide Web access
- Word processing software

**Step 1: Research three major types of broadband Internet connections:**

- DSL
- Cable
- Satellite

**Step 2: Decide which broadband options would be important to you as a teleworker in your small or home office:**

- Cost
- Speed
- Security
- Ease of implementation
- Reliability

**Step 3: Using the options from Step 2, create a matrix that lists the advantages and disadvantages of each broadband type.**

**Step 4: Share your research with the class or another group.**

# 6.2.4.2 Lab – Researching Broadband Internet Access Technologies

## Objectives

**Part 1: Investigate Broadband Distribution**

**Part 2: Research Broadband Access Options for Specific Scenarios**

## Background / Scenario

Although broadband Internet access options have increased dramatically in recent years, broadband access varies greatly depending on location. In this lab, you will investigate current broadband distribution and research broadband access options for specific scenarios.

## Required Resources

Device with Internet access

## Part 1: Investigate Broadband Distribution

In Part 1, you will research broadband distribution in a geographical location.

### Step 1: Research broadband distribution.

Use the Internet to research the following questions:

a. For the country in which you reside, what percentage of the population has broadband Internet subscriptions? _______________

b. What percentage of the population is without broadband Internet options? _______________

### Step 2: Research broadband distribution in the United States.

Navigate to the website www.broadbandmap.gov. The National Broadband Map allows users to search and map broadband availability across the United States.

**Note**: For access options and ISPs for locations outside the United States, perform an Internet search using the keywords "broadband access XYZ, where XYZ is the name of the country.

a. Enter your zip code, city and country that you would like to explore and click **Find Broadband**. List the zip code or city in the space provided. ________________________________________________

b. Click **Show Wired** and **Expand All**. What, if any, wired broadband Internet connections are available at this location? Complete the table below.

| ISP | Connection Type | Download Speed |
|---|---|---|
| | | |
| | | |
| | | |

c. Click **Show Wireless** and **Expand All**. What, if any, wireless broadband Internet connections are available in this location? Complete the table below.

| ISP | Connection Type | Download Speed |
|---|---|---|
| | | |
| | | |
| | | |

d. Return to the home page and click **Explore Map**. The interactive map allows you to explore the geographical availability of a number of broadband Internet options.

e. Highlight each of the wired connections independently (DSL, cable, and fiber). Selections are highlighted in dark blue.

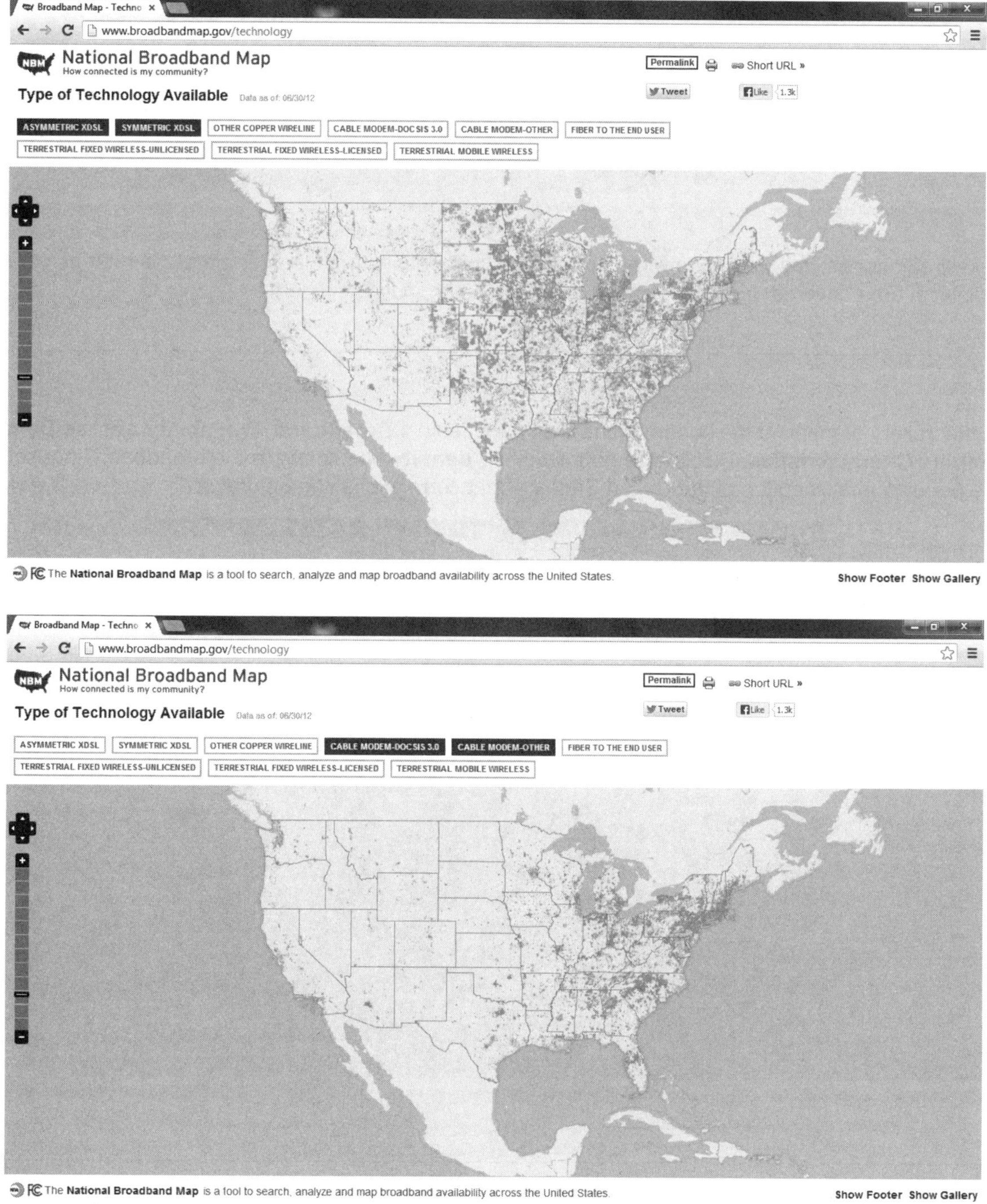

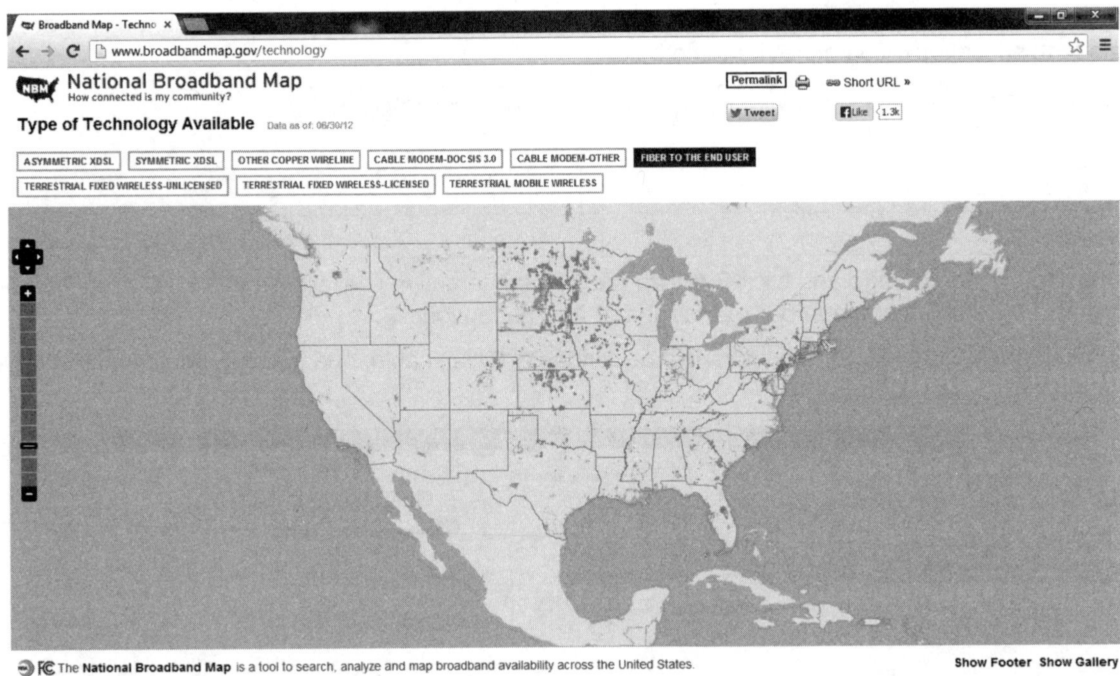


For wired connections, order the wired broadband connections from least to greatest in terms of geographical area covered. List your answer in the space provided.

______________________________________________

f. In the gallery of maps at the bottom of the web page, select **Broadband Availability Across Demographic Characteristics**. Display the population by **density** and compare the broadband connection to the population distribution of the United States. What correlations can be drawn?

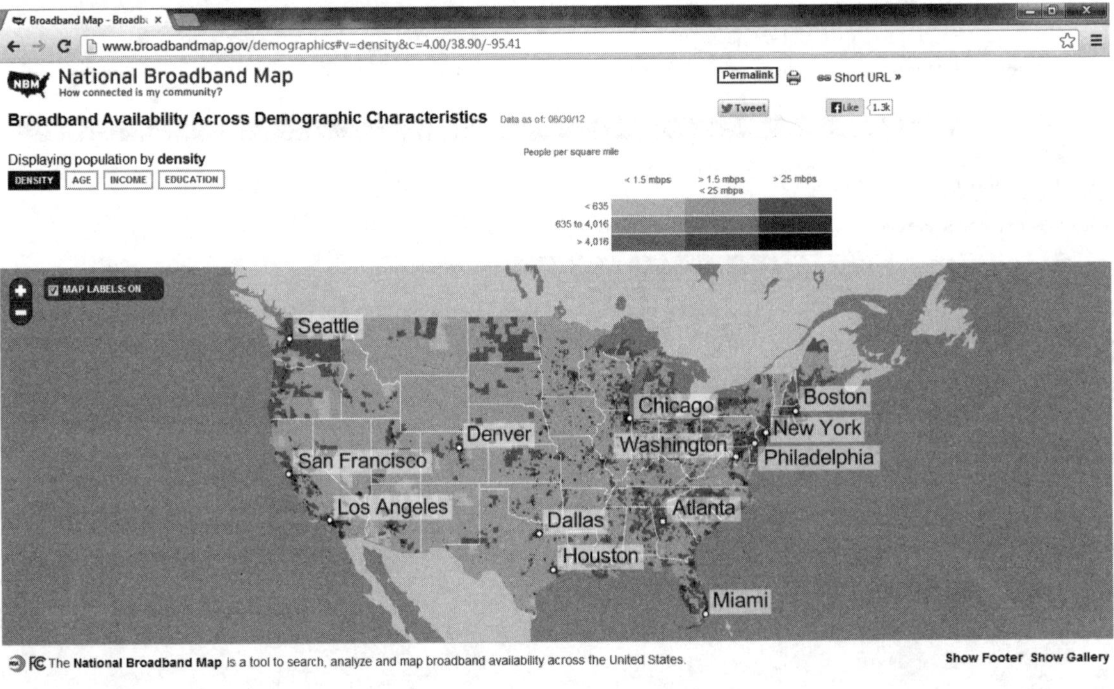


______________________________________________

______________________________________________

______________________________________________

## Part 2: Research Broadband Access Options for Specific Scenarios

In Part 2, you will research and detail broadband options for the following scenarios and select the best last-mile technology to meet the needs of the consumer. You can use the http://www.broadbandmap.gov site as a starting point for your research.

**Scenario 1**: You are moving to Kansas City, Missouri and are exploring home Internet connections. Research and detail two Internet connections from which you can select in this metropolitan area.

| ISP | Connection Type | Cost per Month | Download Speed |
|---|---|---|---|
| | | | |
| | | | |

Choose one from the list of local ISPs that you selected. Give the reasons why you chose that particular ISP.

_______________________________________________

_______________________________________________

_______________________________________________

**Scenario 2**: You are moving to an area outside of Billings, Montana and are exploring home Internet connections. You will be beyond the reach of cable or DSL connections. Research and detail two Internet connections from which you can select in this area.

| ISP | Connection Type | Cost per Month | Download Speed |
|---|---|---|---|
| | | | |
| | | | |

Choose one from the list of local ISPs that you selected. Give the reasons why you chose that particular ISP.

_______________________________________________

_______________________________________________

_______________________________________________

**Scenario 3**: You are moving to New York City and your job requires you to have 24 hours anytime/anywhere access. Research and detail two Internet connections from which you can select in this area.

| ISP | Connection Type | Cost per Month | Download Speed |
|---|---|---|---|
| | | | |
| | | | |

Choose one from the list of local ISPs that you selected. Give the reasons why you chose that particular ISP.

_______________________________________________

_______________________________________________

_______________________________________________

**Scenario 4**: You are small business owner with 10 employees who telecommute in the Fargo, North Dakota area. The teleworkers live beyond the reach of cable Internet connections. Research and detail two Internet connections from which you can select in this area.

| ISP | Connection Type | Cost per Month | Download Speed |
|---|---|---|---|
| | | | |
| | | | |

Choose one from the list of local ISPs that you selected. Give the reasons why you chose that particular ISP.

______________________________

______________________________

______________________________

**Scenario 5**: Your business in Washington, D.C. is expanding to 25 employees and will need to upgrade your broadband access to include equipment colocation and web hosting. Research and detail two Internet connections from which you can select in this area.

| ISP | Connection Type | Cost per Month | Download Speed |
|---|---|---|---|
| | | | |
| | | | |

Choose one from the list of local ISPs that you selected. Give the reasons why you chose that particular ISP.

______________________________

______________________________

______________________________

## Reflection

How do you think broadband Internet access will change in the future?

______________________________

______________________________

______________________________

______________________________

# 6.3.2.3 Lab – Configuring a Router as a PPPoE Client for DSL Connectivity

## Topology

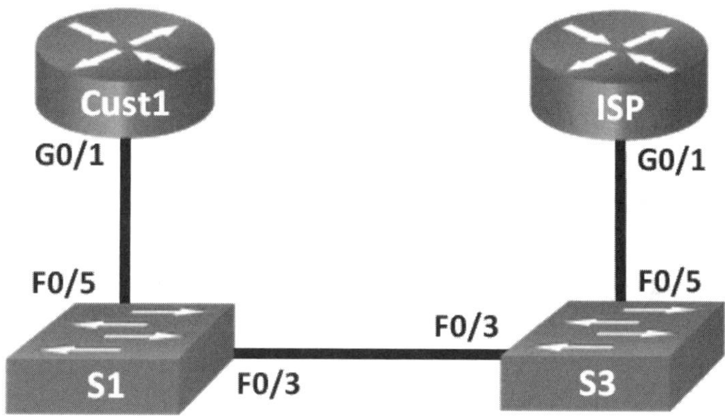


## Addressing Table

| Device | Interface | IP Address | Subnet Mask | Default Gateway |
|---|---|---|---|---|
| Cust1 | G0/1 | Learned via PPP | Learned via PPP | Learned via PPP |
| ISP | G0/1 | N/A | N/A | N/A |

## Objectives

**Part 1: Build the Network**

**Part 2: Configure the ISP Router**

**Part 3: Configure the Cust1 Router**

## Background / Scenario

ISPs often use Point-to-Point Protocol over Ethernet (PPPoE) on DSL links to their customers. PPP supports the assignment of IP address information to a device at the remote end of a PPP link. More importantly, PPP supports CHAP authentication. ISPs can check accounting records to see if a customer's bill has been paid, before letting them connect to the Internet.

In this lab, you will configure both the client and ISP side of the connection to set up PPPoE. Typically, you would only configure the client end.

**Note**: The routers used with CCNA hands-on labs are Cisco 1941 Integrated Services Routers (ISRs) with Cisco IOS Release 15.2(4)M3 (universalk9 image). The switches used are Cisco Catalyst 2960s with Cisco IOS Release 15.0(2) (lanbasek9 image). Other routers, switches, and Cisco IOS versions can be used. Depending on the model and Cisco IOS version, the commands available and output produced might vary from what is shown in the labs. Refer to the Router Interface Summary Table at the end of this lab for the correct interface identifiers.

**Note**: Ensure that the routers and switches have been erased and have no startup configurations. If you are unsure, contact your instructor.

### Required Resources

- 2 Routers (Cisco 1941 with Cisco IOS Release 15.2(4)M3 universal image or comparable)
- 2 Switches (Cisco 2960 with Cisco IOS Release 15.0(2) lanbasek9 image or comparable)
- Console cables to configure the Cisco IOS devices via the console ports
- Ethernet cables as shown in the topology

## Part 1: Build the Network

### Step 1: Cable the network as shown in the topology.

### Step 2: Initialize and reload the routers and switches.

### Step 3: Configure basic settings for each router.

a. Disable DNS lookup.

b. Configure device name as shown in the topology.

c. Encrypt plain text passwords.

d. Create a message of the day (MOTD) banner warning users that unauthorized access is prohibited.

e. Assign **class** as the encrypted privileged EXEC mode password.

f. Assign **cisco** as the console and vty password and enable login.

g. Set console logging to synchronous mode.

h. Save your configuration.

## Part 2: Configure the ISP Router

In Part 2, you configure the ISP router with PPPoE parameters for connection from the Cust1 router.

**Note**: Many of the ISP router PPPoE configuration commands are beyond the scope of the course; however, they are necessary for completion of the lab. They can be copied and pasted into the ISP router at the global configuration mode prompt.

a. Create a local database username **Cust1** with a password of **ciscopppoe**.

```
ISP(config)# username Cust1 password ciscopppoe
```

b. Create a pool of addresses that will be assigned to customers.

```
ISP(config)# ip local pool PPPoEPOOL 10.0.0.1 10.0.0.10
```

c. Create the Virtual Template and associate the IP address of G0/1 with it. Associate the Virtual Template with the pool of addresses. Configure CHAP to authenticate customers.

```
ISP(config)# interface virtual-template 1
ISP(config-if)# ip address 10.0.0.254 255.255.255.0
ISP(config-if)# mtu 1492
ISP(config-if)# peer default ip address pool PPPoEPOOL
ISP(config-if)# ppp authentication chap callin
ISP(config-if)# exit
```

d. Assign the template to the PPPoE group.

```
ISP(config)# bba-group pppoe global
ISP(config-bba-group)# virtual-template 1
ISP(config-bba-group)# exit
```

e. Associate the bba-group with the G0/1 physical interface.

```
ISP(config)# interface g0/1
ISP(config-if# pppoe enable group global
ISP(config-if)# no shutdown
```

# Part 3: Configure the Cust1 Router

In Part 3, you will configure the Cust1 router with PPPoE parameters.

a. Configure G0/1 interface for PPPoE connectivity.

```
Cust1(config)# interface g0/1
Cust1(config-if)# pppoe enable
Cust1(config-if)# pppoe-client dial-pool-number 1
Cust1(config-if)# exit
```

b. Associate the G0/1 interface with a dialer interface. Use the username **Cust1** and password **ciscopppoe** configured in Part 2.

```
Cust1(config)# interface dialer 1
Cust1(config-if)# mtu 1492
Cust1(config-if)# ip address negotiated
Cust1(config-if)# encapsulation ppp
Cust1(config-if)# dialer pool 1
Cust1(config-if)# ppp authentication chap callin
Cust1(config-if)# ppp chap hostname Cust1
Cust1(config-if)# ppp chap password ciscopppoe
Cust1(config-if)# exit
```

c. Set up a static default route pointing to the Dialer interface.

```
Cust1(config)# ip route 0.0.0.0 0.0.0.0 dialer 1
```

d. Set up debugging on the Cust1 router to display PPP and PPPoE negotiation.

```
Cust1# debug ppp authentication
Cust1# debug pppoe events
```

e. Enable the G0/1 interface on the Cust1 router and observe the debug output as the PPPoE dialer session is established and CHAP authentication takes place.

```
*Jul 30 19:28:42.427: %LINK-3-UPDOWN: Interface GigabitEthernet0/1, changed state to
down
*Jul 30 19:28:46.175: %LINK-3-UPDOWN: Interface GigabitEthernet0/1, changed state to
up
*Jul 30 19:28:47.175: %LINEPROTO-5-UPDOWN: Line protocol on Interface
GigabitEthernet0/1, changed state to up
*Jul 30 19:29:03.839:  padi timer expired
*Jul 30 19:29:03.839:  Sending PADI: Interface = GigabitEthernet0/1
*Jul 30 19:29:03.839: PPPoE 0: I PADO  R:30f7.0da3.0b01 L:30f7.0da3.0bc1 Gi0/1
*Jul 30 19:29:05.887:  PPPOE: we've got our pado and the pado timer went off
*Jul 30 19:29:05.887: OUT PADR from PPPoE Session
*Jul 30 19:29:05.895: PPPoE 1: I PADS  R:30f7.0da3.0b01 L:30f7.0da3.0bc1 Gi0/1
*Jul 30 19:29:05.895: IN PADS from PPPoE Session
*Jul 30 19:29:05.899: %DIALER-6-BIND: Interface Vi2 bound to profile Di1
*Jul 30 19:29:05.899: PPPoE: Virtual Access interface obtained.
```

```
*Jul 30 19:29:05.899: PPPoE : encap string prepared
*Jul 30 19:29:05.899: [0]PPPoE 1: data path set to PPPoE Client
*Jul 30 19:29:05.903: %LINK-3-UPDOWN: Interface Virtual-Access2, changed state to up
*Jul 30 19:29:05.911: Vi2 PPP: Using dialer call direction
*Jul 30 19:29:05.911: Vi2 PPP: Treating connection as a callout
*Jul 30 19:29:05.911: Vi2 PPP: Session handle[C6000001] Session id[1]
*Jul 30 19:29:05.919: Vi2 PPP: No authorization without authentication
*Jul 30 19:29:05.939: Vi2 CHAP: I CHALLENGE id 1 len 24 from "ISP"
*Jul 30 19:29:05.939: Vi2 PPP: Sent CHAP SENDAUTH Request
*Jul 30 19:29:05.939: Vi2 PPP: Received SENDAUTH Response FAIL
*Jul 30 19:29:05.939: Vi2 CHAP: Using hostname from interface CHAP
*Jul 30 19:29:05.939: Vi2 CHAP: Using password from interface CHAP
*Jul 30 19:29:05.939: Vi2 CHAP: O RESPONSE id 1 len 26 from "Cust1"
*Jul 30 19:29:05.955: Vi2 CHAP: I SUCCESS id 1 len 4
*Jul 30 19:29:05.955: %LINEPROTO-5-UPDOWN: Line protocol on Interface Virtual-Access2,
changed state to up
*Jul 30 19:29:05.983: PPPoE : ipfib_encapstr  prepared
*Jul 30 19:29:05.983: PPPoE : ipfib_encapstr  prepared
```

f. Issue a **show ip interface brief** command on the Cust1 router to display the IP address assigned by the ISP router. Sample output is shown below. By what method was the IP address obtained?

____________________

```
Cust1# show ip interface brief
Interface                  IP-Address      OK? Method Status                Protocol
Embedded-Service-Engine0/0 unassigned      YES unset  administratively down down
GigabitEthernet0/0         unassigned      YES unset  administratively down down
GigabitEthernet0/1         unassigned      YES unset  up                    up
Serial0/0/0                unassigned      YES unset  administratively down down
Serial0/0/1                unassigned      YES unset  administratively down down
Dialer1                    10.0.0.1        YES IPCP   up                    up
Virtual-Access1            unassigned      YES unset  up                    up
Virtual-Access2            unassigned      YES unset  up                    up
```

g. Issue a **show ip route** command on the Cust1 router. Sample output is shown below.

```
Cust1# show ip route
Codes: L - local, C - connected, S - static, R - RIP, M - mobile, B - BGP
       D - EIGRP, EX - EIGRP external, O - OSPF, IA - OSPF inter area
       N1 - OSPF NSSA external type 1, N2 - OSPF NSSA external type 2
       E1 - OSPF external type 1, E2 - OSPF external type 2
       i - IS-IS, su - IS-IS summary, L1 - IS-IS level-1, L2 - IS-IS level-2
       ia - IS-IS inter area, * - candidate default, U - per-user static route
       o - ODR, P - periodic downloaded static route, H - NHRP, l - LISP
       + - replicated route, % - next hop override

Gateway of last resort is 0.0.0.0 to network 0.0.0.0

S*    0.0.0.0/0 is directly connected, Dialer1
      10.0.0.0/32 is subnetted, 2 subnets
C        10.0.0.1 is directly connected, Dialer1
C        10.0.0.254 is directly connected, Dialer1
```

h. Issue a **show pppoe session** on Cust1 router. Sample output is shown below.

```
Cust1# show pppoe session
     1 client session

Uniq ID  PPPoE  RemMAC          Port                    VT  VA          State
           SID  LocMAC                                      VA-st       Type
    N/A      1  30f7.0da3.0b01  Gi0/1                   Di1 Vi2         UP
                30f7.0da3.0bc1                              UP
```

i. Issue a ping to 10.0.0.254 from the Cust1 router. The ping should be successful. If not, troubleshoot until you have connectivity.

```
Cust1# ping 10.0.0.254
Type escape sequence to abort.
Sending 5, 100-byte ICMP Echos to 10.0.0.254, timeout is 2 seconds:
!!!!!
Success rate is 100 percent (5/5), round-trip min/avg/max = 1/1/4 ms
```

## Reflection

Why do ISPs who use DSL, primarily use PPPoE with their customers?

_______________________________________________

## Router Interface Summary Table

| Router Interface Summary | | | | |
|---|---|---|---|---|
| **Router Model** | **Ethernet Interface #1** | **Ethernet Interface #2** | **Serial Interface #1** | **Serial Interface #2** |
| 1800 | Fast Ethernet 0/0 (F0/0) | Fast Ethernet 0/1 (F0/1) | Serial 0/0/0 (S0/0/0) | Serial 0/0/1 (S0/0/1) |
| 1900 | Gigabit Ethernet 0/0 (G0/0) | Gigabit Ethernet 0/1 (G0/1) | Serial 0/0/0 (S0/0/0) | Serial 0/0/1 (S0/0/1) |
| 2801 | Fast Ethernet 0/0 (F0/0) | Fast Ethernet 0/1 (F0/1) | Serial 0/1/0 (S0/1/0) | Serial 0/1/1 (S0/1/1) |
| 2811 | Fast Ethernet 0/0 (F0/0) | Fast Ethernet 0/1 (F0/1) | Serial 0/0/0 (S0/0/0) | Serial 0/0/1 (S0/0/1) |
| 2900 | Gigabit Ethernet 0/0 (G0/0) | Gigabit Ethernet 0/1 (G0/1) | Serial 0/0/0 (S0/0/0) | Serial 0/0/1 (S0/0/1) |
| **Note**: To find out how the router is configured, look at the interfaces to identify the type of router and how many interfaces the router has. There is no way to effectively list all the combinations of configurations for each router class. This table includes identifiers for the possible combinations of Ethernet and Serial interfaces in the device. The table does not include any other type of interface, even though a specific router may contain one. An example of this might be an ISDN BRI interface. The string in parenthesis is the legal abbreviation that can be used in Cisco IOS commands to represent the interface. | | | | |

# 6.4.1.1 Class Activity – Telework Proposal

## Objective

Describe the business requirements of teleworking.

## Scenario

Your small- to medium-sized business has just been awarded a large marketing design contract. Because your office space is limited, it has been decided that it would be a good idea to hire teleworkers to help with the contract.

Therefore, a very general teleworking program must be designed for your company due to anticipation of company growth. As more contracts are awarded, you will revise and expand the program to fit your company's needs.

Develop a basic telework proposal outline for your company to consider as groundwork for a telework program.

## Resources

- World Wide Web access
- Word processing software

### Step 1: Research documented telework programs using the Internet.

a. Notate information found to be important to established telework programs and record the source URL's of this research.

b. At a minimum, include the following proposal areas:

   1) Telework tasks to be considered.

   2) Employee selection methods to be used.

   3) Equipment that may be needed by the teleworker.

   4) Possible communication methods.

   5) Techniques that could be used to evaluate the telework program.

### Step 2: Design a basic telework program requirements outline.

### Step 3: Share your proposal with another student, the class, or another group.

# Chapter 7 — Securing Site-to-Site Connectivity

## 7.0.1.2 Class Activity – VPNs at a Glance

### Objective

Explain the use of VPNs in securing site-to-site connectivity in a small- to medium-sized business network.

### Scenario

A small- to medium-sized business is growing and needs customers, teleworkers, and wired/wireless employees to be able to access the main network from any location. As the network administrator for the business, you have decided to implement VPNs for security, network access ease, and cost savings.

It is your job to ensure that all of the network administrators start the VPN planning process with the same knowledge set.

Four basic VPN informational areas need to be researched and presented to the network administrative team:

- Concise definition of VPNs
- Some general VPN facts
- IPsec as a VPN security option
- Ways VPNs use tunneling

### Resources

- World Wide Web access
- Word processing or presentation software

### Directions

**Step 1: Individual students research all four of the following topics and take notes on their research:**

a. Topic 1: A concise definition of VPNs
b. Topic 2: Five general facts about VPNs
c. Topic 3: IPsec defined as a security option when using VPNs
d. Topic 4: A graphic showing how VPNs use tunneling

**Step 2: After students research their topics, groups of four students will be formed to discuss their individual research.**

a. Each group will agree on
   1) One concise VPN definition
   2) Five facts describing VPNs
   3) One definition of IPsec as a VPN security option
   4) One graphic showing a VPN network using tunneling

**Step 3: Each group will design a four-slide presentation (one slide per topic) to deliver to the class for discussion.**

# 7.2.2.5 Lab – Configuring a Point-to-Point GRE VPN Tunnel

## Topology

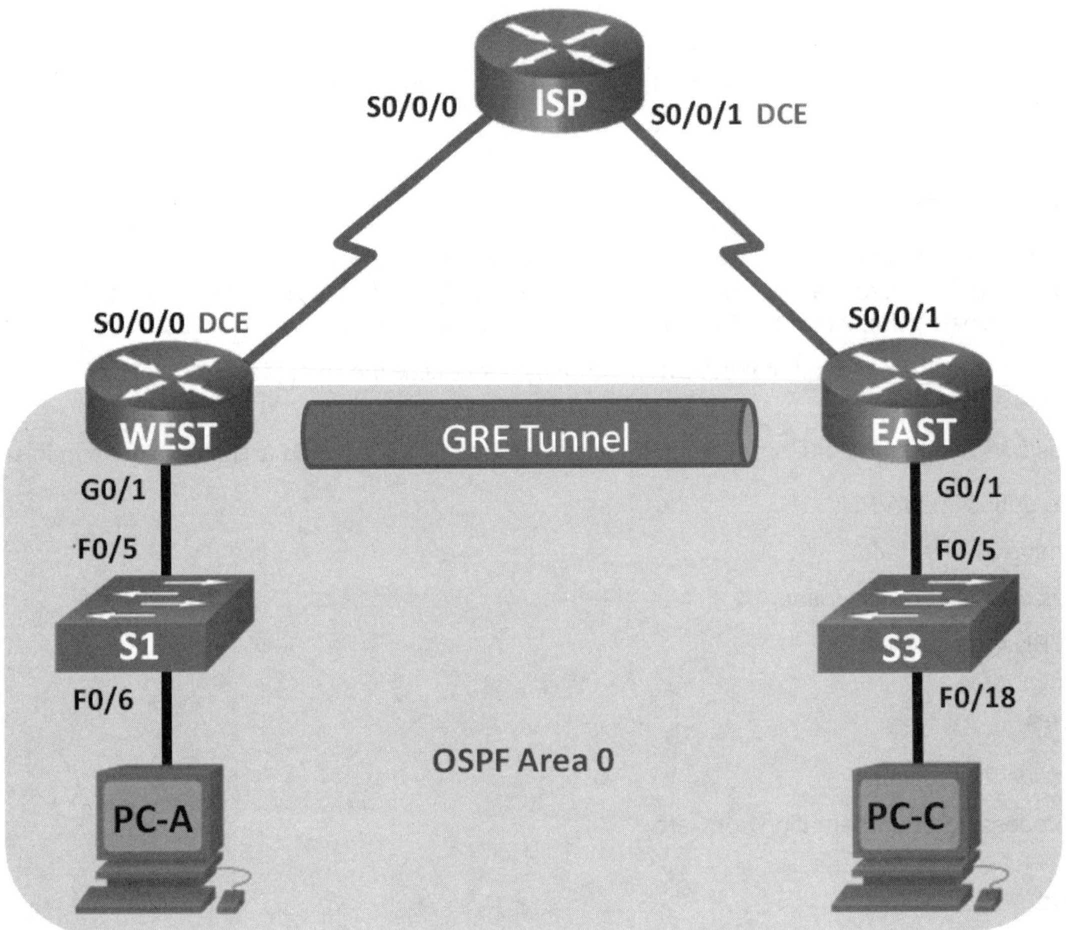


## Addressing Table

| Device | Interface | IP Address | Subnet Mask | Default Gateway |
|---|---|---|---|---|
| WEST | G0/1 | 172.16.1.1 | 255.255.255.0 | N/A |
| | S0/0/0 (DCE) | 10.1.1.1 | 255.255.255.252 | N/A |
| | Tunnel0 | 172.16.12.1 | 255.255.255.252 | N/A |
| ISP | S0/0/0 | 10.1.1.2 | 255.255.255.252 | N/A |
| | S0/0/1 (DCE) | 10.2.2.2 | 255.255.255.252 | N/A |
| EAST | G0/1 | 172.16.2.1 | 255.255.255.0 | N/A |
| | S0/0/1 | 10.2.2.1 | 255.255.255.252 | N/A |
| | Tunnel0 | 172.16.12.2 | 255.255.255.252 | N/A |
| PC-A | NIC | 172.16.1.3 | 255.255.255.0 | 172.16.1.1 |
| PC-C | NIC | 172.16.2.3 | 255.255.255.0 | 172.16.2.1 |

## Objectives

**Part 1: Configure Basic Device Settings**

**Part 2: Configure a GRE Tunnel**

**Part 3: Enable Routing over the GRE Tunnel**

## Background / Scenario

Generic Routing Encapsulation (GRE) is a tunneling protocol that can encapsulate a variety of network layer protocols between two locations over a public network, such as the Internet.

GRE can be used with:

- Connecting IPv6 networks over IPv4 networks
- Multicast packets, such as OSPF, EIGRP, and streaming applications

In this lab, you will configure an unencrypted point-to-point GRE VPN tunnel and verify that network traffic is using the tunnel. You will also configure the OSPF routing protocol inside the GRE VPN tunnel. The GRE tunnel is between the WEST and EAST routers in OSPF area 0. The ISP has no knowledge of the GRE tunnel. Communication between the WEST and EAST routers and the ISP is accomplished using default static routes.

**Note**: The routers used with CCNA hands-on labs are Cisco 1941 Integrated Services Routers (ISRs) with Cisco IOS Release 15.2(4)M3 (universalk9 image). The switches used are Cisco Catalyst 2960s with Cisco IOS Release 15.0(2) (lanbasek9 image). Other routers, switches, and Cisco IOS versions can be used. Depending on the model and Cisco IOS version, the commands available and output produced might vary from what is shown in the labs. Refer to the Router Interface Summary Table at the end of this lab for the correct interface identifiers.

**Note**: Make sure that the routers and switches have been erased and have no startup configurations. If you are unsure, contact your instructor.

## Required Resources

- 3 Routers (Cisco 1941 with Cisco IOS Release 15.2(4)M3 universal image or comparable)
- 2 Switches (Cisco 2960 with Cisco IOS Release 15.0(2) lanbasek9 image or comparable)
- 2 PCs (Windows 7, Vista, or XP with terminal emulation program, such as Tera Term)
- Console cables to configure the Cisco IOS devices via the console ports
- Ethernet and serial cables as shown in the topology

# Part 1: Configure Basic Device Settings

In Part 1, you will set up the network topology and configure basic router settings, such as the interface IP addresses, routing, device access, and passwords.

### Step 1: Cable the network as shown in the topology.

### Step 2: Initialize and reload the routers and switches.

### Step 3: Configure basic settings for each router.

a. Disable DNS lookup.

b. Configure the device names.

c. Encrypt plain text passwords.

d. Create a message of the day (MOTD) banner warning users that unauthorized access is prohibited.

e. Assign **class** as the encrypted privileged EXEC mode password.

f. Assign **cisco** as the console and vty password and enable login.

g. Set console logging to synchronous mode.

h. Apply IP addresses to Serial and Gigabit Ethernet interfaces according to the Addressing Table and activate the physical interfaces. Do NOT configure the Tunnel0 interfaces at this time.

i. Set the clock rate to **128000** for DCE serial interfaces.

### Step 4: Configure default routes to the ISP router.

```
WEST(config)# ip route 0.0.0.0 0.0.0.0 10.1.1.2

EAST(config)# ip route 0.0.0.0 0.0.0.0 10.2.2.2
```

### Step 5: Configure the PCs.

Assign IP addresses and default gateways to the PCs according to the Addressing Table.

### Step 6: Verify connectivity.

At this point, the PCs are unable to ping each other. Each PC should be able to ping its default gateway. The routers are able to ping the serial interfaces of the other routers in the topology. If not, troubleshoot until you can verify connectivity.

### Step 7: Save your running configuration.

## Part 2: Configure a GRE Tunnel

In Part 2, you will configure a GRE tunnel between the WEST and EAST routers.

### Step 1: Configure the GRE tunnel interface.

a. Configure the tunnel interface on the WEST router. Use S0/0/0 on WEST as the tunnel source interface and 10.2.2.1 as the tunnel destination on the EAST router.

```
WEST(config)# interface tunnel 0
WEST(config-if)# ip address 172.16.12.1 255.255.255.252
WEST(config-if)# tunnel source s0/0/0
WEST(config-if)# tunnel destination 10.2.2.1
```

b. Configure the tunnel interface on the EAST router. Use S0/0/1 on EAST as the tunnel source interface and 10.1.1.1 as the tunnel destination on the WEST router.

```
EAST(config)# interface tunnel 0
EAST(config-if)# ip address 172.16.12.2 255.255.255.252
EAST(config-if)# tunnel source 10.2.2.1
EAST(config-if)# tunnel destination 10.1.1.1
```

**Note**: For the **tunnel source** command, either the interface name or the IP address can be used as the source.

## Step 2: Verify that the GRE tunnel is functional.

a. Verify the status of the tunnel interface on the WEST and EAST routers.

```
WEST# show ip interface brief
Interface                  IP-Address      OK? Method Status                Protocol
Embedded-Service-Engine0/0 unassigned      YES unset  administratively down down
GigabitEthernet0/0         unassigned      YES unset  administratively down down
GigabitEthernet0/1         172.16.1.1      YES manual up                    up
Serial0/0/0                10.1.1.1        YES manual up                    up
Serial0/0/1                unassigned      YES unset  administratively down down
Tunnel0                    172.16.12.1     YES manual up                    up

EAST# show ip interface brief
Interface                  IP-Address      OK? Method Status                Protocol
Embedded-Service-Engine0/0 unassigned      YES unset  administratively down down
GigabitEthernet0/0         unassigned      YES unset  administratively down down
GigabitEthernet0/1         172.16.2.1      YES manual up                    up
Serial0/0/0                unassigned      YES unset  administratively down down
Serial0/0/1                10.2.2.1        YES manual up                    up
Tunnel0                    172.16.12.2     YES manual up                    up
```

b. Issue the **show interfaces tunnel 0** command to verify the tunneling protocol, tunnel source, and tunnel destination used in this tunnel.

What is the tunneling protocol used? What are the tunnel source and destination IP addresses associated with GRE tunnel on each router?

____________________________________________________________________________

____________________________________________________________________________

c. Ping across the tunnel from the WEST router to the EAST router using the IP address of the tunnel interface.

```
WEST# ping 172.16.12.2
Type escape sequence to abort.
Sending 5, 100-byte ICMP Echos to 172.16.12.2, timeout is 2 seconds:
!!!!!
Success rate is 100 percent (5/5), round-trip min/avg/max = 32/34/36 ms
```

d. Use the **traceroute** command on the WEST to determine the path to the tunnel interface on the EAST router. What is the path to the EAST router?

____________________________________________________

e. Ping and trace the route across the tunnel from the EAST router to the WEST router using the IP address of the tunnel interface.

What is the path to the WEST router from the EAST router? ____________________________

With which interfaces are these IP addresses associated? Why? ____________________________

____________________________________________________

____________________________________________________________________________

f. The **ping** and **traceroute** commands should be successful. If not, troubleshoot before continuing to the next part.

## Part 3: Enable Routing over the GRE Tunnel

In Part 3, you will configure OSPF routing so that the LANs on the WEST and EAST routers can communicate using the GRE tunnel.

After the GRE tunnel is set up, the routing protocol can be implemented. For GRE tunneling, a network statement will include the IP network of the tunnel, instead of the network associated with the serial interface. just like you would with other interfaces, such as Serial and Ethernet. Remember that the ISP router is not participating in this routing process.

### Step 1: Configure OSPF routing for area 0 over the tunnel.

a. Configure OSPF process ID 1 using area 0 on the WEST router for the 172.16.1.0/24 and 172.16.12.0/24 networks.

```
WEST(config)# router ospf 1
WEST(config-router)# network 172.16.1.0 0.0.0.255 area 0
WEST(config-router)# network 172.16.12.0 0.0.0.3 area 0
```

b. Configure OSPF process ID 1 using area 0 on the EAST router for the 172.16.2.0/24 and 172.16.12.0/24 networks.

```
EAST(config)# router ospf 1
EAST(config-router)# network 172.16.2.0 0.0.0.255 area 0
EAST(config-router)# network 172.16.12.0 0.0.0.3 area 0
```

### Step 2: Verify OSPF routing.

a. From the WEST router, issue the **show ip route** command to verify the route to 172.16.2.0/24 LAN on the EAST router.

```
WEST# show ip route
Codes: L - local, C - connected, S - static, R - RIP, M - mobile, B - BGP
       D - EIGRP, EX - EIGRP external, O - OSPF, IA - OSPF inter area
       N1 - OSPF NSSA external type 1, N2 - OSPF NSSA external type 2
       E1 - OSPF external type 1, E2 - OSPF external type 2
       i - IS-IS, su - IS-IS summary, L1 - IS-IS level-1, L2 - IS-IS level-2
       ia - IS-IS inter area, * - candidate default, U - per-user static route
       o - ODR, P - periodic downloaded static route, H - NHRP, l - LISP
       + - replicated route, % - next hop override

Gateway of last resort is 10.1.1.2 to network 0.0.0.0

S*    0.0.0.0/0 [1/0] via 10.1.1.2
      10.0.0.0/8 is variably subnetted, 2 subnets, 2 masks
C        10.1.1.0/30 is directly connected, Serial0/0/0
L        10.1.1.1/32 is directly connected, Serial0/0/0
      172.16.0.0/16 is variably subnetted, 5 subnets, 3 masks
C        172.16.1.0/24 is directly connected, GigabitEthernet0/1
L        172.16.1.1/32 is directly connected, GigabitEthernet0/1
O        172.16.2.0/24 [110/1001] via 172.16.12.2, 00:00:07, Tunnel0
C        172.16.12.0/30 is directly connected, Tunnel0
L        172.16.12.1/32 is directly connected, Tunnel0
```

What is the exit interface and IP address to reach the 172.16.2.0/24 network?

____________________________________________________________

b. From the EAST router issue the command to verify the route to 172.16.1.0/24 LAN on the WEST router.

   What is the exit interface and IP address to reach the 172.16.1.0/24 network?

   ____________________________________________

### Step 3: Verify end-to-end connectivity.

a. Ping from PC-A to PC-C. It should be successful. If not, troubleshoot until you have end-to-end connectivity.

   **Note**: It may be necessary to disable the PC firewall to ping between PCs.

b. Traceroute from PC-A to PC-C. What is the path from PC-A to PC-C?

   ____________________________________________

## Reflection

1. What other configurations are needed to create a secured GRE tunnel?

   ____________________________________________

2. If you added more LANs to the WEST or EAST router, what would you need to do so that the network will use the GRE tunnel for traffic?

   ____________________________________________

## Router Interface Summary Table

| Router Interface Summary | | | | |
|---|---|---|---|---|
| **Router Model** | **Ethernet Interface #1** | **Ethernet Interface #2** | **Serial Interface #1** | **Serial Interface #2** |
| 1800 | Fast Ethernet 0/0 (F0/0) | Fast Ethernet 0/1 (F0/1) | Serial 0/0/0 (S0/0/0) | Serial 0/0/1 (S0/0/1) |
| 1900 | Gigabit Ethernet 0/0 (G0/0) | Gigabit Ethernet 0/1 (G0/1) | Serial 0/0/0 (S0/0/0) | Serial 0/0/1 (S0/0/1) |
| 2801 | Fast Ethernet 0/0 (F0/0) | Fast Ethernet 0/1 (F0/1) | Serial 0/1/0 (S0/1/0) | Serial 0/1/1 (S0/1/1) |
| 2811 | Fast Ethernet 0/0 (F0/0) | Fast Ethernet 0/1 (F0/1) | Serial 0/0/0 (S0/0/0) | Serial 0/0/1 (S0/0/1) |
| 2900 | Gigabit Ethernet 0/0 (G0/0) | Gigabit Ethernet 0/1 (G0/1) | Serial 0/0/0 (S0/0/0) | Serial 0/0/1 (S0/0/1) |
| **Note**: To find out how the router is configured, look at the interfaces to identify the type of router and how many interfaces the router has. There is no way to effectively list all the combinations of configurations for each router class. This table includes identifiers for the possible combinations of Ethernet and Serial interfaces in the device. The table does not include any other type of interface, even though a specific router may contain one. An example of this might be an ISDN BRI interface. The string in parenthesis is the legal abbreviation that can be used in Cisco IOS commands to represent the interface. | | | | |

# 7.5.1.1 Class Activity – VPN Planning Design

## Objective

Explain the use of VPNs in securing site-to-site connectivity in a small- to medium-sized business network.

## Scenario

Your small- to medium-sized business has received quite a few new contracts lately. This has increased the need for teleworkers and workload outsourcing. The new contract vendors and clients will also need access to your network as the projects progress.

As network administrator for the business, you recognize that VPNs must be incorporated as a part of your network strategy to support secure access by the teleworkers, employees, and vendors or clients.

To prepare for implementation of VPNs on the network, you devise a planning checklist to bring to the next department meeting for discussion.

## Resources

- World Wide Web access
- Packet Tracer software
- Word processing software

### Step 1: Visit the VPN Discovery Tool, or any other Internet site with VPN-implementation, or planning checklist examples.

### Step 2: Use Packet Tracer to draw the current topology for your network; no device configurations are necessary. Include:

- Two branch offices: the Internet cloud and one headquarters location
- Current network devices: servers, switches, routers/core routers, broadband ISR devices, and local user workstations

### Step 3: On the Packet Tracer topology, indicate:

a. Where you would implement VPNs?

b. What types of VPNs would be needed?

   1) Site to site

   2) Remote access

### Step 4: Using a word processing software program, create a small VPN planning checklist based on your research from Step 1.

### Step 5: Share your work with the class, another group, or your instructor.

# Chapter 8 — Monitoring the Network

## 8.0.1.2 Class Activity – Network Maintenance Development

### Objective

Describe the different levels of router log messages.

### Scenario

Currently, there are no formal policies or procedures for recording problems experienced on your company's network. Furthermore, when network problems occur, you must try many methods to find the causes – and this troubleshooting approach takes time.

You know there must be a better way to resolve these issues. You decide to create a network maintenance plan to keep repair records and pinpoint the causes of errors on the network.

### Resources

- Word processing software

### Directions

**Step 1: Brainstorm different types of network maintenance records you would like to keep.**

**Step 2: Sort the records types into main categories. Suggested categories include:**

- Equipment (Routers and Switches)
- Traffic
- Security

**Step 3: Create an outline to guide the network maintenance planning process for the company.**

# 8.1.2.6 Lab – Configuring Syslog and NTP

## Topology

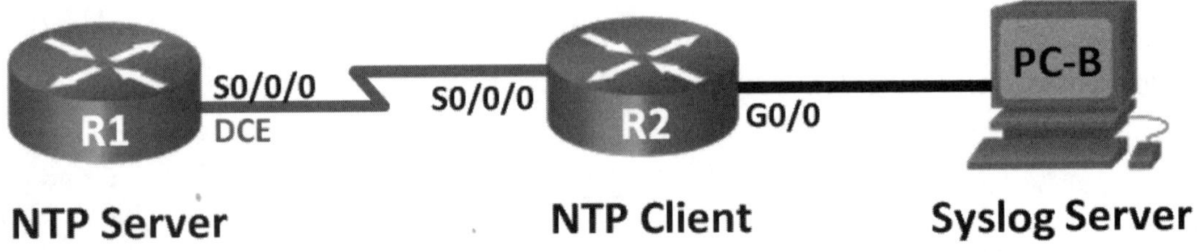


## Addressing Table

| Device | Interface | IP Address | Subnet Mask | Default Gateway |
|---|---|---|---|---|
| R1 | S0/0/0 (DCE) | 10.1.1.1 | 255.255.255.252 | N/A |
| R2 | S0/0/0 | 10.1.1.2 | 255.255.255.252 | N/A |
| | G0/0 | 172.16.2.1 | 255.255.255.0 | N/A |
| PC-B | NIC | 172.16.2.3 | 255.255.255.0 | 172.16.2.1 |

## Objectives

**Part 1: Configure Basic Device Settings**

**Part 2: Configure NTP**

**Part 3: Configure Syslog**

## Background / Scenario

Syslog messages that are generated by the network devices can be collected and archived on a syslog server. The information can be used for monitoring, debugging, and troubleshooting purposes. The administrator can control where the messages are stored and displayed. Syslog messages can be time-stamped for analysis of the sequence of network events; therefore, it is important to synchronize the clock across the network devices with a Network Time Protocol (NTP) server.

In this lab, you will configure R1 as the NTP server and R2 as a Syslog and NTP client. The syslog server application, such as Tftp32d or other similar program, will be running on PC-B. Furthermore, you will control the severity level of log messages that are collected and archived on the syslog server.

**Note**: The routers used with CCNA hands-on labs are Cisco 1941 Integrated Services Routers (ISRs) with Cisco IOS Release 15.2(4)M3 (universalk9 image). Other routers and Cisco IOS versions can be used. Depending on the model and Cisco IOS version, the commands available and output produced might vary from what is shown in the labs. Refer to the Router Interface Summary Table at the end of this lab for the correct interface identifiers.

**Note**: Make sure that the routers have been erased and have no startup configurations. If you are unsure, contact your instructor.

## Required Resources

- 2 Routers (Cisco 1941 with Cisco IOS Release 15.2(4)M3 universal image or comparable)
- 1 PC (Windows 7, Vista, or XP with terminal emulation program, such as Tera Term, and Syslog software, such as tftpd32)
- Console cables to configure the Cisco IOS devices via the console ports
- Ethernet and serial cables as shown in the topology

# Part 1: Configure Basic Device Settings

In Part 1, you will set up the network topology and configure basic settings, such as the interface IP addresses, routing, device access, and passwords.

### Step 1: Cable the network as shown in the topology.

### Step 2: Initialize and reload the routers as necessary.

### Step 3: Configure basic settings for each router.

a. Disable DNS lookup.

b. Configure the device name.

c. Encrypt plain text passwords.

d. Create a message of the day (MOTD) banner warning users that unauthorized access is prohibited.

e. Assign **class** as the encrypted privileged EXEC mode password.

f. Assign **cisco** as the console and vty password and enable login.

g. Set console logging to synchronous mode.

h. Apply the IP addresses to Serial and Gigabit Ethernet interfaces according to the Addressing Table and activate the physical interfaces.

i. Set the clock rate to **128000** for the DCE serial interface.

### Step 4: Configure routing.

Enable single-area OSPF on the routers with process ID 1. Add all the networks into the OSPF process for area 0.

### Step 5: Configure PC-B.

Configure the IP address and default gateway for PC-B according to the Addressing Table.

### Step 6: Verify end-to-end connectivity.

Verify that each device is able to ping every other device in the network successfully. If not, troubleshoot until there is end-to-end connectivity.

### Step 7: Save the running configuration to the startup configuration.

## Part 2: Configure NTP

In Part 2, you will configure R1 as the NTP server and R2 as the NTP client of R1. Synchronized time is important for syslog and debug functions. If the time is not synchronized, it is difficult to determine what network event caused the message.

### Step 1: Display the current time.

Issue the **show clock** command to display the current time on R1.

```
R1# show clock
*12:30:06.147 UTC Tue May 14 2013
```

Record the information regarding the current time displayed in the following table.

| Date | |
|---|---|
| Time | |
| Time Zone | |

### Step 2: Set the time.

Use the **clock set** command to set the time on R1. The following is an example of setting the date and time.

```
R1# clock set 9:39:00 05 july 2013
R1#
*Jul  5 09:39:00.000: %SYS-6-CLOCKUPDATE: System clock has been updated from 12:30:54
UTC Tue May 14 2013 to 09:39:00 UTC Fri Jul 5 2013, configured from console by console.
```

**Note**: The time can also be set using the **clock timezone** command in the global configuration mode. For more information regarding this command, research the **clock timezone** command at www.cisco.com to determine the zone for your region.

### Step 3: Configure the NTP master.

Configure R1 as the NTP master by using the **ntp master** *stratum-number* command in global configuration mode. The stratum number indicates the number of NTP hops away from an authoritative time source. In this lab, the number 5 is the stratum level of this NTP server.

```
R1(config)# ntp master 5
```

### Step 4: Configure the NTP client.

a. Issue **show clock** command on R2. Record the current time displayed on R2 in the following table.

| Date | |
|---|---|
| Time | |
| Time Zone | |

b. Configure R2 as the NTP client. Use the **ntp server** command to point to the IP address or hostname of the NTP server. The **ntp update-calendar** command periodically updates the calendar with NTP time.

```
R2(config)# ntp server 10.1.1.1
R2(config)# ntp update-calendar
```

### Step 5: Verify NTP configuration.

a. Use the **show ntp associations** command to verify that R2 has an NTP association with R1.

```
R2# show ntp associations

  address         ref clock       st   when   poll reach  delay  offset   disp
*~10.1.1.1        127.127.1.1      5     11     64   177 11.312  -0.018  4.298
 * sys.peer, # selected, + candidate, - outlyer, x falseticker, ~ configured
```

b. Issue **show clock** on R1 and R2 to compare the timestamp.

**Note**: It could take a few minutes before the timestamp on R2 is synchronized with R1.

```
R1# show clock
09:43:32.799 UTC Fri Jul 5 2013
R2# show clock
09:43:37.122 UTC Fri Jul 5 2013
```

## Part 3: Configure Syslog

Syslog messages from network devices can be collected and archived on a syslog server. In this lab, Tftpd32 will be used as the syslog server software. The network administrator can control the types of messages that can be sent to the syslog server.

### Step 1: (Optional) Install syslog server.

If a syslog server is not already installed on the PC, download and install the latest version of a syslog server, such as Tftpd32, on the PC. The latest version of Tftpd32 can be found at the following link:

http://tftpd32.jounin.net/

### Step 2: Start the syslog server on PC-B.

After starting the Tftpd32 application, click the **syslog server** tab.

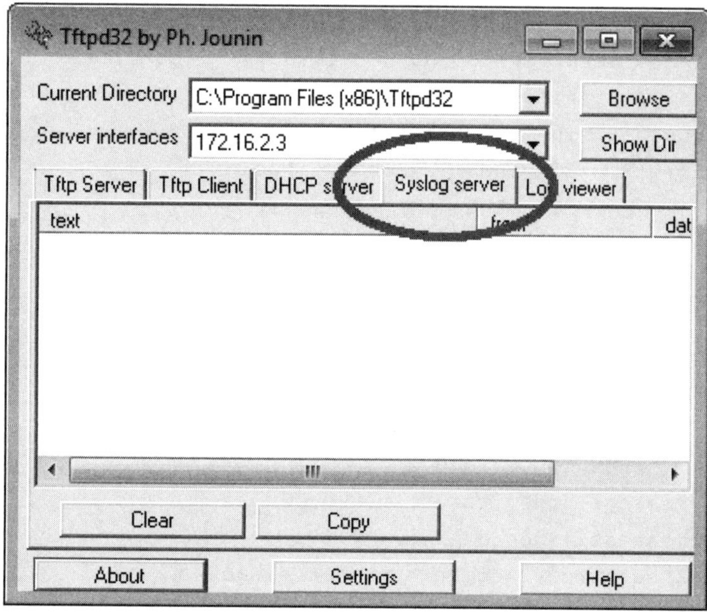

### Step 3: Verify that the timestamp service is enabled on R2.

Use the **show run** command to verify that the timestamp service is enabled for logging on R2.

```
R2# show run | include timestamp
service timestamps debug datetime msec
service timestamps log datetime msec
```

If the timestamp service is not enabled, use the following command to enable it.

```
R2(config)# service timestamps log datetime msec
```

### Step 4: Configure R2 to log messages to the syslog server.

Configure R2 to send Syslog messages to the syslog server, PC-B. The IP address of the PC-B syslog server is 172.16.2.3.

```
R2(config)# logging host 172.16.2.3
```

### Step 5: Display the default logging settings.

Use the **show logging** command to display the default logging settings.

```
R2# show logging
Syslog logging: enabled (0 messages dropped, 2 messages rate-limited, 0 flushes, 0
overruns, xml disabled, filtering disabled)

No Active Message Discriminator.


No Inactive Message Discriminator.


    Console logging: level debugging, 47 messages logged, xml disabled,
                     filtering disabled
    Monitor logging: level debugging, 0 messages logged, xml disabled,
                     filtering disabled
    Buffer logging:  level debugging, 47 messages logged, xml disabled,
                    filtering disabled
    Exception Logging: size (4096 bytes)
    Count and timestamp logging messages: disabled
    Persistent logging: disabled

No active filter modules.

    Trap logging: level informational, 49 message lines logged
        Logging to 172.16.2.3  (udp port 514, audit disabled,
              link up),
              6 message lines logged,
              0 message lines rate-limited,
              0 message lines dropped-by-MD,
              xml disabled, sequence number disabled
              filtering disabled
        Logging Source-Interface:       VRF Name:
```

What is the IP address of the syslog server? ____________________

What protocol and port is syslog using? ____________________

At what level is trap logging enabled? ____________________

### Step 6: Configure and observe the effect of logging severity levels on R2.

a. Use the **logging trap ?** command to determine the various trap levels availability. When configuring a level, the messages sent to the syslog server are the trap level configured and any lower levels.

```
R2(config)# logging trap ?
  <0-7>          Logging severity level
  alerts         Immediate action needed           (severity=1)
  critical       Critical conditions               (severity=2)
  debugging      Debugging messages                (severity=7)
  emergencies    System is unusable                (severity=0)
  errors         Error conditions                  (severity=3)
  informational  Informational messages            (severity=6)
  notifications  Normal but significant conditions (severity=5)
  warnings       Warning conditions                (severity=4)
  <cr>
```

If the **logging trap warnings** command was issued, which severity levels of messages are logged?

________________________________________

b. Change the logging severity level to 4.

```
R2(config)# logging trap warnings
```

or

```
R2(config)# logging trap 4
```

c. Create interface Loopback0 on R2 and observe the log messages on both the terminal window and the syslog server window on PC-B.

```
R2(config)# interface lo 0
R2(config-if)#
Jul  5 09:57:47.162: %LINK-3-UPDOWN: Interface Loopback0, changed state to up
Jul  5 09:57:48.162: %LINEPROTO-5-UPDOWN: Line protocol on Interface Loopback0,
changed state to up
```

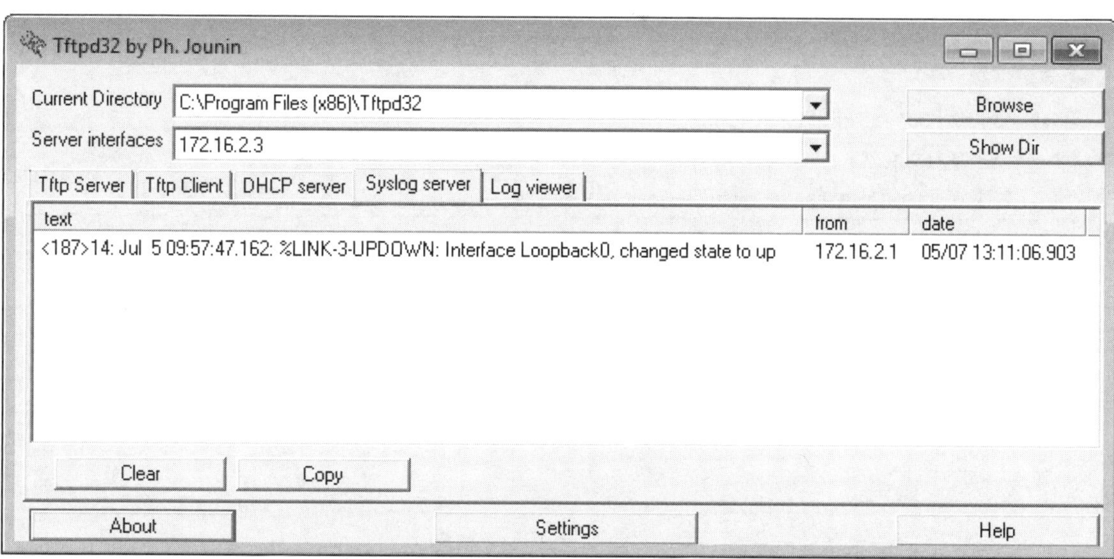

d. Remove the Loopback 0 interface on R2 and observe the log messages.

```
R2(config-if)# no interface lo 0
R2(config)#
Jul  5 10:02:58.910: %LINK-5-CHANGED: Interface Loopback0, changed state to
administratively down
Jul  5 10:02:59.910: %LINEPROTO-5-UPDOWN: Line protocol on Interface Loopback0,
changed state to down
```

At severity level 4, are there any log messages on the syslog server? If any log messages appeared, explain what appeared and why.

____________________________________________

____________________________________________

____________________________________________

____________________________________________

e. Change the logging severity level to 6.

```
R2(config)# logging trap informational
```

or

```
R2(config)# logging trap 6
```

f. Clear the syslog entries on PC-B. Click **Clear** in the Tftpd32 dialog box.

g. Create the Loopback 1 interface on R2.

```
R2(config)# interface lo 1
Jul  5 10:05:46.650: %LINK-3-UPDOWN: Interface Loopback1, changed state to up
Jul  5 10:05:47.650: %LINEPROTO-5-UPDOWN: Line protocol on Interface Loopback1,
changed state to up
```

h. Remove the Loopback 1 interface from R2.

```
R2(config-if)# no interface lo 1
R2(config-if)#
Jul  5 10:08:29.742: %LINK-5-CHANGED: Interface Loopback1, changed state to
administratively down
Jul  5 10:08:30.742: %LINEPROTO-5-UPDOWN: Line protocol on Interface Loopback1,
changed state to down
```

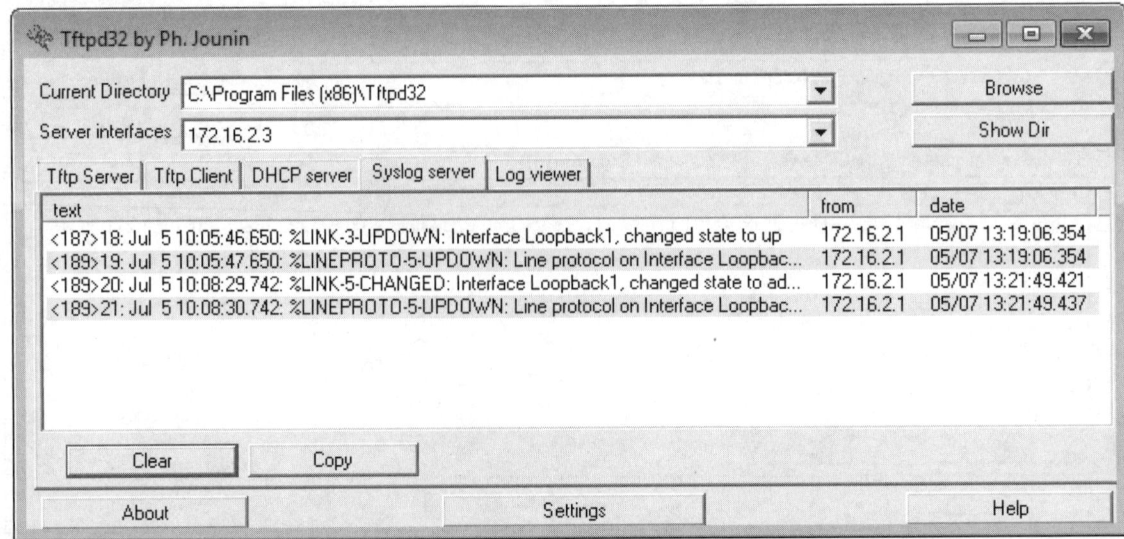

i. Observe the syslog server output. Compare this result with the results at trapping level 4. What is your observation?

____________________________________________________________

____________________________________________________________

____________________________________________________________

## Reflection

What is the problem with setting the level of severity too high (lowest level number) or too low (highest level number) for syslog?

____________________________________________________________

____________________________________________________________

____________________________________________________________

## Router Interface Summary Table

| Router Interface Summary | | | | |
|---|---|---|---|---|
| **Router Model** | **Ethernet Interface #1** | **Ethernet Interface #2** | **Serial Interface #1** | **Serial Interface #2** |
| 1800 | Fast Ethernet 0/0 (F0/0) | Fast Ethernet 0/1 (F0/1) | Serial 0/0/0 (S0/0/0) | Serial 0/0/1 (S0/0/1) |
| 1900 | Gigabit Ethernet 0/0 (G0/0) | Gigabit Ethernet 0/1 (G0/1) | Serial 0/0/0 (S0/0/0) | Serial 0/0/1 (S0/0/1) |
| 2801 | Fast Ethernet 0/0 (F0/0) | Fast Ethernet 0/1 (F0/1) | Serial 0/1/0 (S0/1/0) | Serial 0/1/1 (S0/1/1) |
| 2811 | Fast Ethernet 0/0 (F0/0) | Fast Ethernet 0/1 (F0/1) | Serial 0/0/0 (S0/0/0) | Serial 0/0/1 (S0/0/1) |
| 2900 | Gigabit Ethernet 0/0 (G0/0) | Gigabit Ethernet 0/1 (G0/1) | Serial 0/0/0 (S0/0/0) | Serial 0/0/1 (S0/0/1) |
| **Note**: To find out how the router is configured, look at the interfaces to identify the type of router and how many interfaces the router has. There is no way to effectively list all the combinations of configurations for each router class. This table includes identifiers for the possible combinations of Ethernet and Serial interfaces in the device. The table does not include any other type of interface, even though a specific router may contain one. An example of this might be an ISDN BRI interface. The string in parenthesis is the legal abbreviation that can be used in Cisco IOS commands to represent the interface. | | | | |

# 8.2.1.8 Lab – Researching Network Monitoring Software

## Objectives

**Part 1: Survey Your Understanding of Network Monitoring**

**Part 2: Research Network Monitoring Tools**

**Part 3: Select a Network Monitoring Tool**

## Background / Scenario

Network monitoring is needed for any sized network. Proactively monitoring the network infrastructure can assist network administrators with their day-to-day duties. The wide variety of networking tools available vary in cost, depending on the features, number of network locations and number of nodes supported.

In this lab, you will conduct research on available network monitoring software. You will gather information on software products and features of those products. You will investigate one product in greater detail and list some of the key features available.

## Required Resources

- PC with Internet access

## Part 1: Survey Your Understanding of Network Monitoring

Describe network monitoring as you understand it. Give an example of how it might be used in a production network.

______________________________________________________________________

______________________________________________________________________

______________________________________________________________________

______________________________________________________________________

______________________________________________________________________

______________________________________________________________________

## Part 2: Research Network Monitoring Tools

### Step 1: Research and find three network monitoring tools.

List the three tools that you found.

______________________________________________________________________

______________________________________________________________________

______________________________________________________________________

### Step 2: Complete the following form for the network monitoring tools selected.

| Vendor | Product Name | Features |
|---|---|---|
| | | |
| | | |
| | | |

## Part 3: Select a Network Monitoring Tool

### Step 1: Select one or more monitoring tools from your research.

From your research, identify one or more tools you would choose for monitoring your network. List the tools and explain your reasons for choosing them, including specific features that you consider important.

______________________________________________________________________

______________________________________________________________________

______________________________________________________________________

______________________________________________________________________

______________________________________________________________________

______________________________________________________________________

### Step 2: Investigate the PRTG network monitoring tool.

Navigate to www.paessler.com/prtg.

Give examples of some of the features that you found for PRTG in the space provided below.

______________________________________________________________________

______________________________________________________________________

______________________________________________________________________

______________________________________________________________________

______________________________________________________________________

______________________________________________________________________

## Reflection

Based on your research, what conclusions have you reached regarding network monitoring software?

______________________________________________________________________

______________________________________________________________________

______________________________________________________________________

______________________________________________________________________

# 8.2.2.4 Lab – Configuring SNMP

## Topology

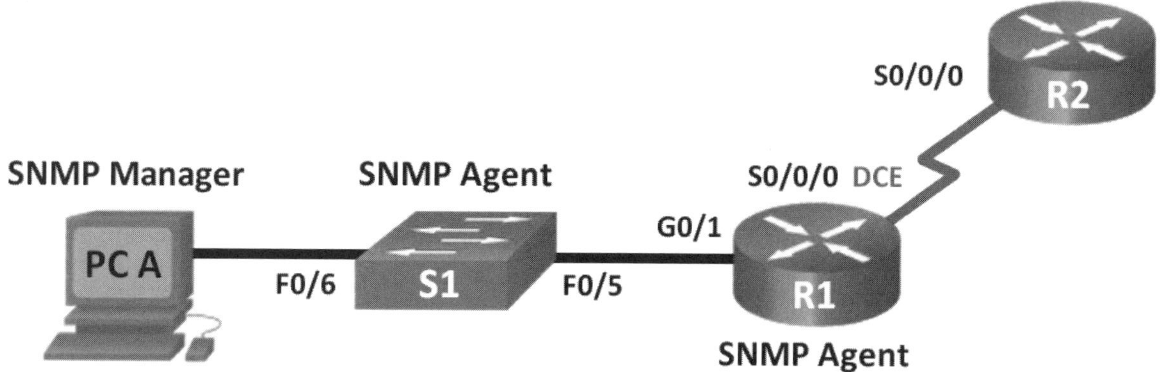


## Addressing Table

| Device | Interface | IP Address | Subnet Mask | Default Gateway |
|---|---|---|---|---|
| R1 | G0/1 | 192.168.1.1 | 255.255.255.0 | N/A |
| | S0/0/0 | 192.168.2.1 | 255.255.255.252 | N/A |
| R2 | S0/0/0 | 192.168.2.2 | 255.255.255.252 | N/A |
| S1 | VLAN 1 | 192.168.1.2 | 255.255.255.0 | N/A |
| PC-A | NIC | 192.168.1.3 | 255.255.255.0 | 192.168.1.1 |

## Objectives

**Part 1: Build the Network and Configure Basic Device Settings**

**Part 2: Configure an SNMP Manager and Agents**

**Part 3: Convert OID Codes with the Cisco SNMP Object Navigator**

## Background / Scenario

Simple Network Management Protocol (SNMP) is a network management protocol and an IETF standard which can be used to both monitor and control clients on the network. SNMP can be used to get and set variables related to the status and configuration of network hosts like routers and switches, as well as network client computers. The SNMP manager can poll SNMP agents for data, or data can be automatically sent to the SNMP manager by configuring traps on the SNMP agents.

In this lab, you will download, install, and configure SNMP management software on PC-A. You will also configure a Cisco router and Cisco switch as SNMP agents. After capturing SNMP notification messages from the SNMP agent, you will convert the MIB/Object ID codes to learn the details of the messages using the Cisco SNMP Object Navigator.

**Note**: The routers used with CCNA hands-on labs are Cisco 1941 Integrated Services Routers (ISRs) with Cisco IOS Release 15.2(4)M3 (universalk9 image). The switches used are Cisco Catalyst 2960s with Cisco IOS Release 15.0(2) (lanbasek9 image). Other routers, switches and Cisco IOS versions can be used. Depending on the model and Cisco IOS version, the commands available and output produced might vary from what is shown in the labs. Refer to the Router Interface Summary Table at the end of the lab for the correct interface identifiers.

**Note**: Make sure that the routers and switches have been erased and have no startup configurations. If you are unsure, contact your instructor.

**Note**: The **snmp-server** commands in this lab will cause the Cisco 2960 switch to issue a warning message when saving the configuration file to NVRAM. To avoid this warning message verify that the switch is using the **lanbase-routing** template. The IOS template is controlled by the Switch Database Manager (SDM). When changing the preferred template, the new template will be used after reboot even if the configuration is not saved.

```
S1# show sdm prefer
```

Use the following commands to assign the **lanbase-routing** template as the default SDM template.

```
S1# configure terminal
S1(config)# sdm prefer lanbase-routing
S1(config)# end
S1# reload
```

## Required Resources

- 2 Routers (Cisco 1941 with Cisco IOS, Release 15.2(4)M3 universal image or comparable)
- 1 Switch (Cisco 2960 with Cisco IOS Release 15.0(2) lanbasek9 image or comparable)
- 1 PC (Windows 7, Vista, or XP with terminal emulation program, such as Tera Term)
- 1 PC (Windows 7, Vista, or XP with Internet access)
- Console cables to configure the Cisco IOS devices via the console ports
- Ethernet and serial cables as shown in the topology
- SNMP Management Software (PowerSNMP Free Manager by Dart Communications, or SolarWinds Kiwi Syslog Server, Evaluation Version with 30 Day Trial)

# Part 1: Build the Network and Configure Basic Device Settings

In Part 1, you will set up the network topology and configure the devices with basic settings.

### Step 1: Cable the network as shown in the topology.

### Step 2: Configure the PC host.

### Step 3: Initialize and reload the switch and routers as necessary.

### Step 4: Configure basic settings for the routers and switch.

a. Disable DNS lookup.

b. Configure device names as shown in the topology.

c. Configure IP addresses as shown in the Addressing Table. (Do not configure the S0/0/0 interface on R1 at this time.)

d. Assign **cisco** as the console and vty password and enable login.

e. Assign **class** as the encrypted privileged EXEC mode password.

f. Configure **logging synchronous** to prevent console messages from interrupting command entry.

g. Verify successful connectivity between the LAN devices by issuing the ping command.

h. Copy the running configuration to the startup configuration.

## Part 2: Configure SNMP Manager and Agents

In Part 2, SNMP management software will be installed and configured on PC-A, and R1 and S1 will be configured as SNMP agents.

### Step 1: Install an SNMP management program.

a. Download and install the PowerSNMP Free Manager by Dart Communications from the following URL: http://www.dart.com/snmp-free-manager.aspx.

b. Launch the PowerSNMP Free Manager program.

c. Click **No** if prompted to discover available SNMP agents. You will discover SNMP agents after configuring SNMP on R1. PowerSNMP Free Manager supports SNMP version 1, 2, and 3. This lab uses SNMPv2.

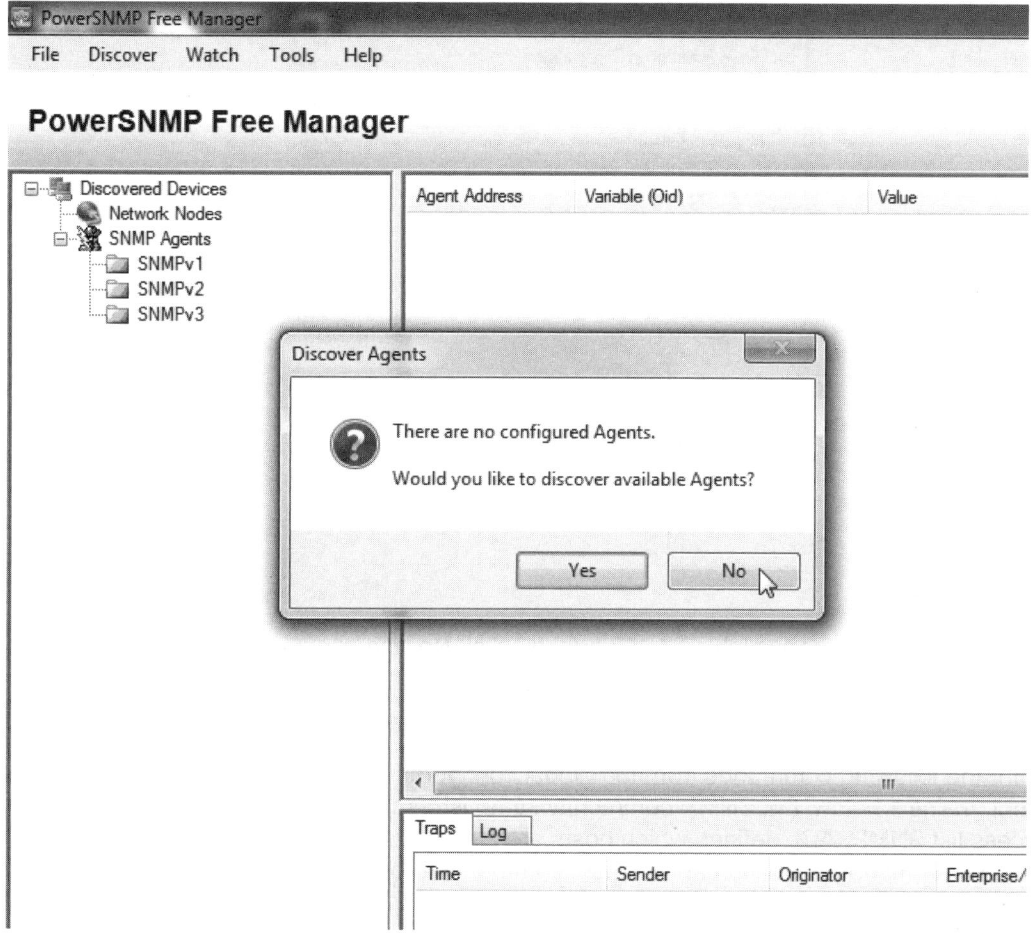


d. In the pop-up Configuration window (if no pop-up window appear, go to Tools > Configuration), set the local IP address to listen on 192.168.1.3 and click **OK**.

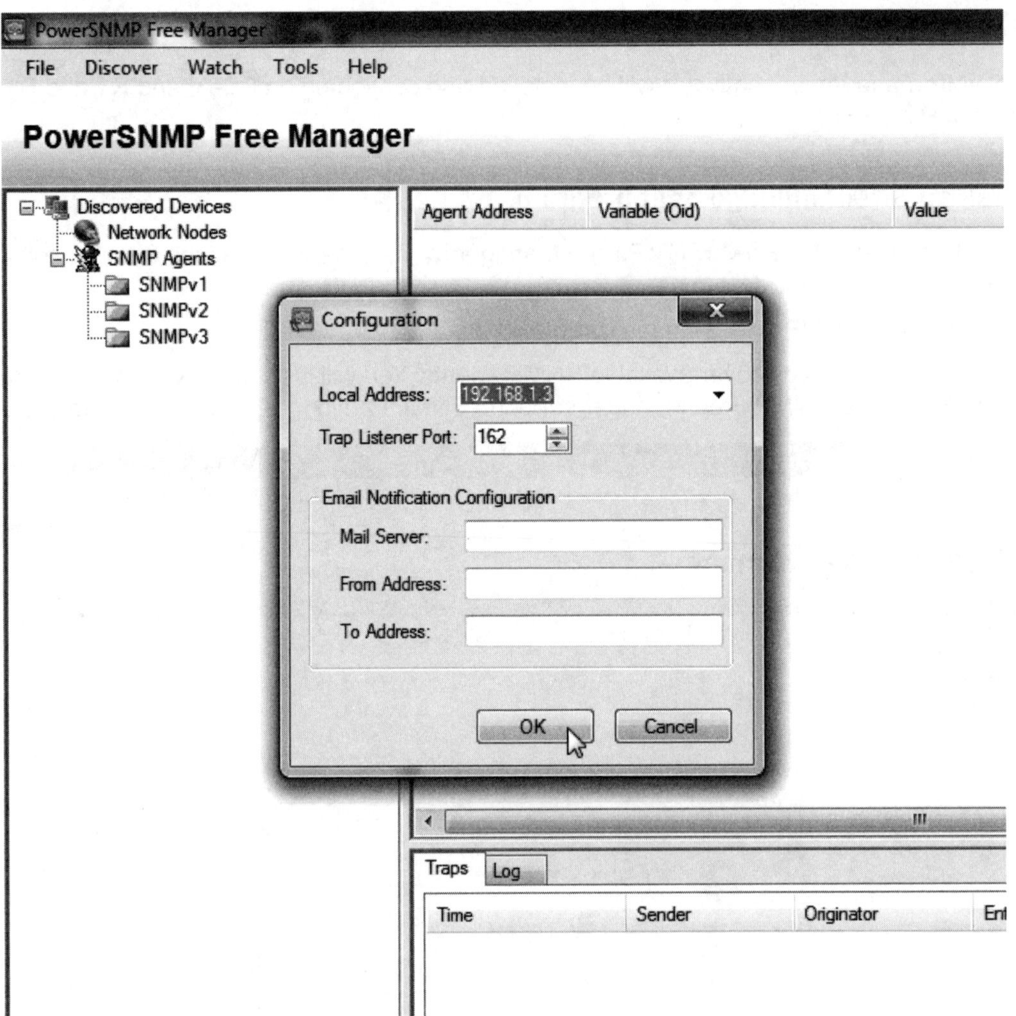


**Note**: If prompted to discover available SNMP agents, click **No** and continue to next part of the lab.

### Step 2: Configure an SNMP agent.

a. On R1, enter the following commands from the global configuration mode to configure the router as an SNMP agent. In line 1 below, the SNMP community string is **ciscolab**, with read-only privileges, and the named access list SNMP_ACL defines which hosts are allowed to get SNMP information from R1. In lines 2 and 3, the SNMP manager location and contact commands provide descriptive contact information. Line 4 specifies the IP address of the host that will receive SNMP notifications, the SNMP version, and the community string. Line 5 enables all default SNMP traps, and lines 6 and 7 create the named access list, to control which hosts are permitted to get SNMP information from the router.

```
R1(config)# snmp-server community ciscolab ro SNMP_ACL
R1(config)# snmp-server location snmp_manager
R1(config)# snmp-server contact ciscolab_admin
R1(config)# snmp-server host 192.168.1.3 version 2c ciscolab
R1(config)# snmp-server enable traps
R1(config)# ip access-list standard SNMP_ACL
R1(config-std-nacl)# permit 192.168.1.3
```

b. At this point, you may notice that the PowerSNMP Free Manager is receiving notifications from R1. If it is not, you can try to force a SNMP notification to be sent by entering a **copy run start** command on R1. Continue to the next step if it is unsuccessful.

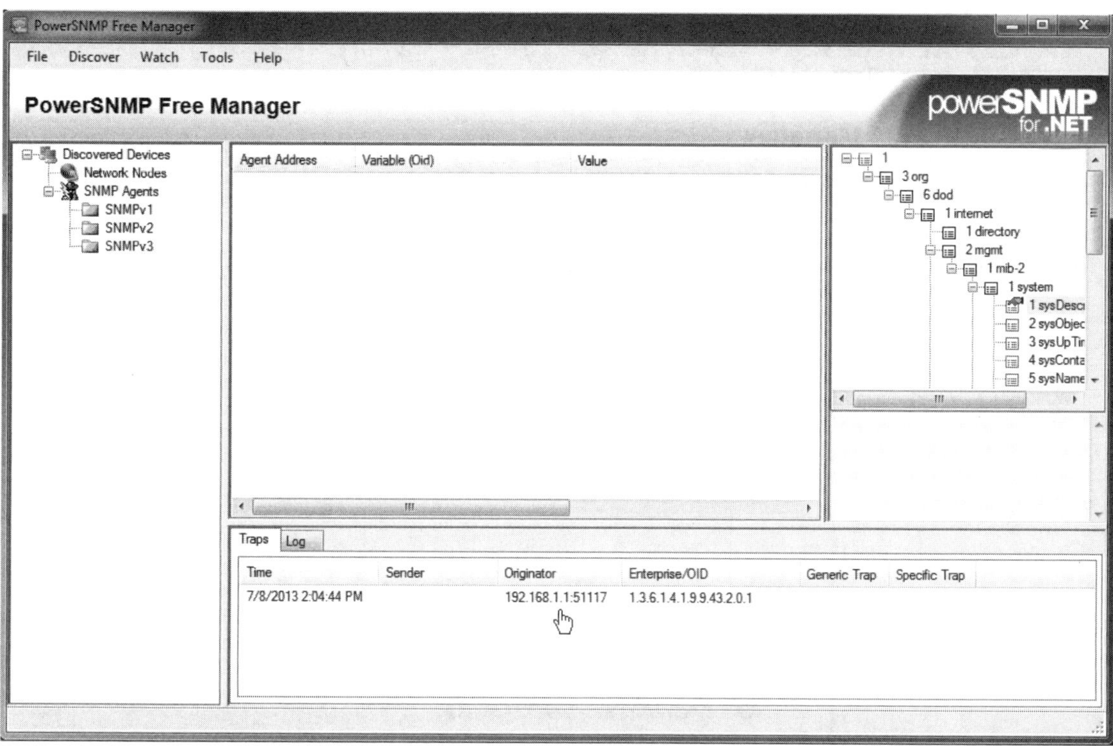


## Step 3: Discover SNMP agents.

a. From the PowerSNMP Free Manager on PC-A, open the **Discover > SNMP Agents** window. Enter the IP address **192.168.1.255**. In the same window, click **Properties** and set the Community to **ciscolab** and the SNMP Version to **Two**, and then click **OK**. Now you can click **Find** to discover all SNMP agents on the 192.168.1.0 network. The PowerSNMP Free Manager should find R1 at 192.168.1.1. Click the checkbox and then **Add** to add R1 as an SNMP agent.

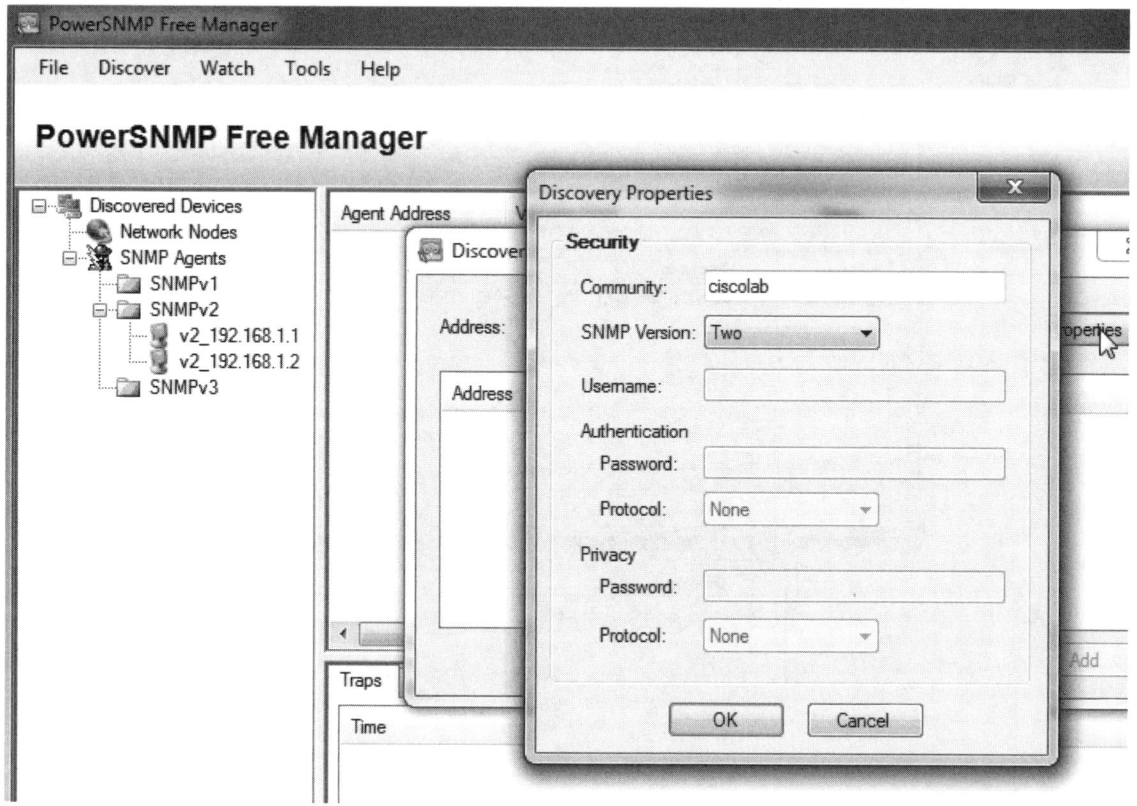

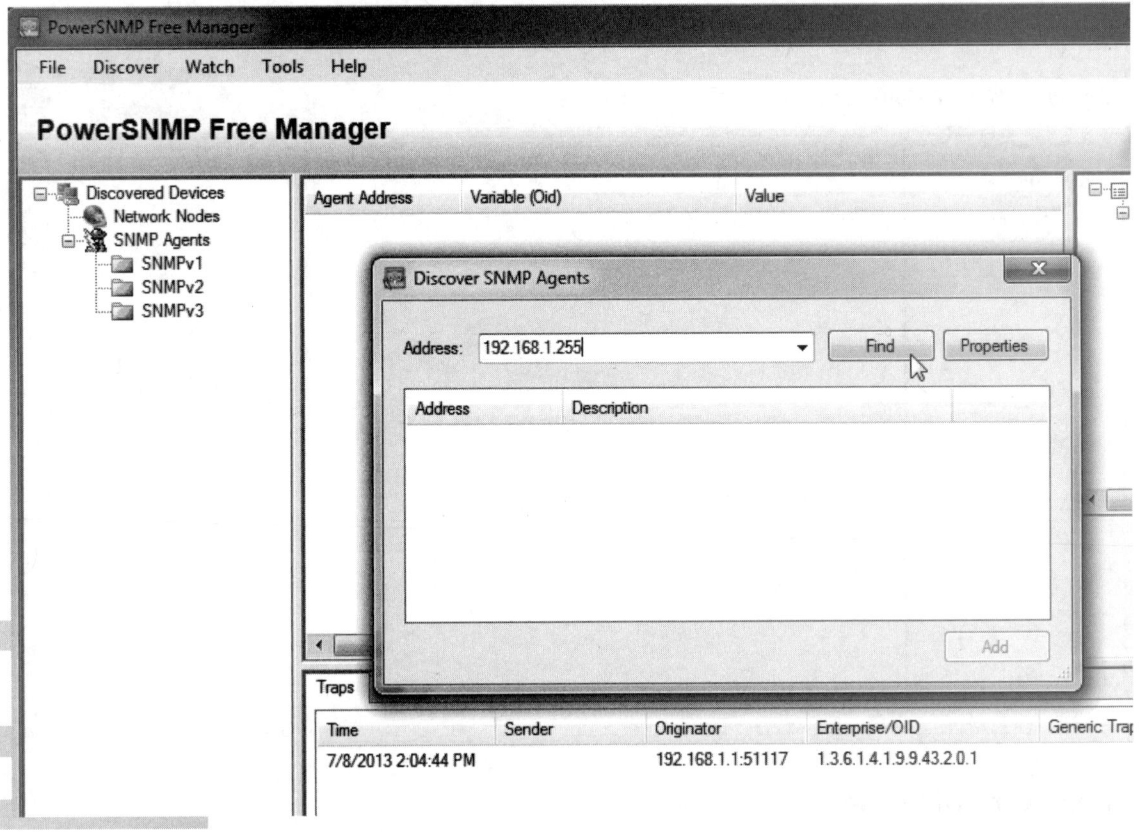
PowerSNMP Free Manager
File
Discover
Watch
Tools
Help
PowerSNMP Free Manager
Discovered Devices
Network Nodes
SNMP Agents
SNMPv1
SNMPv2
SNMPv3
Agent Address
Variable (Oid)
Value
Discover SNMP Agents
Address:
192.168.1.255
Find
Properties
Address
Description
Add
Traps
Time
Sender
Originator
Enterprise/OID
7/8/2013 2:04:44 PM
192.168.1.1:51117
1.3.6.1.4.1.9.9.43.2.0.1

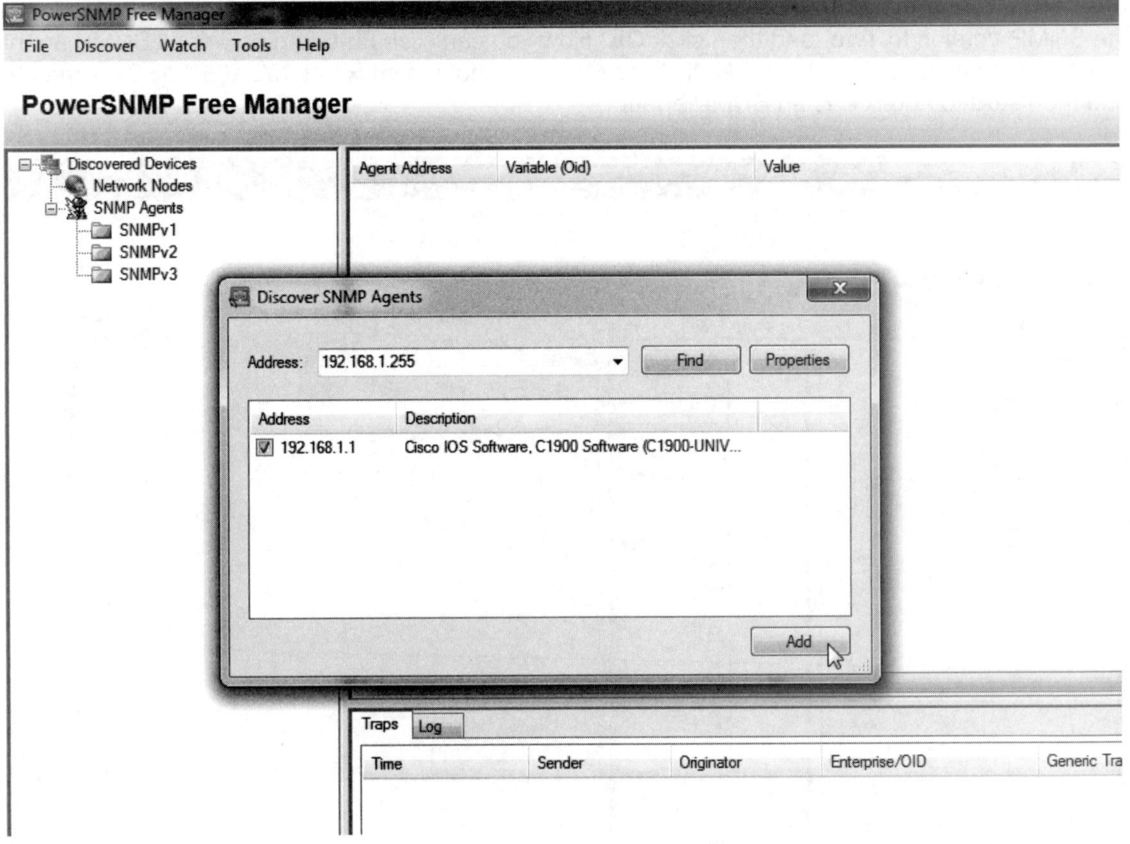
PowerSNMP Free Manager
File
Discover
Watch
Tools
Help
PowerSNMP Free Manager
Discovered Devices
Network Nodes
SNMP Agents
SNMPv1
SNMPv2
SNMPv3
Agent Address
Variable (Oid)
Value
Discover SNMP Agents
Address:
192.168.1.255
Find
Properties
Address
Description
192.168.1.1
Cisco IOS Software, C1900 Software (C1900-UNIV...
Add
Traps
Log
Time
Sender
Originator
Enterprise/OID

b. In the PowerSNMP Free Manager, R1 is added to the list of available SNMPv2 agents.

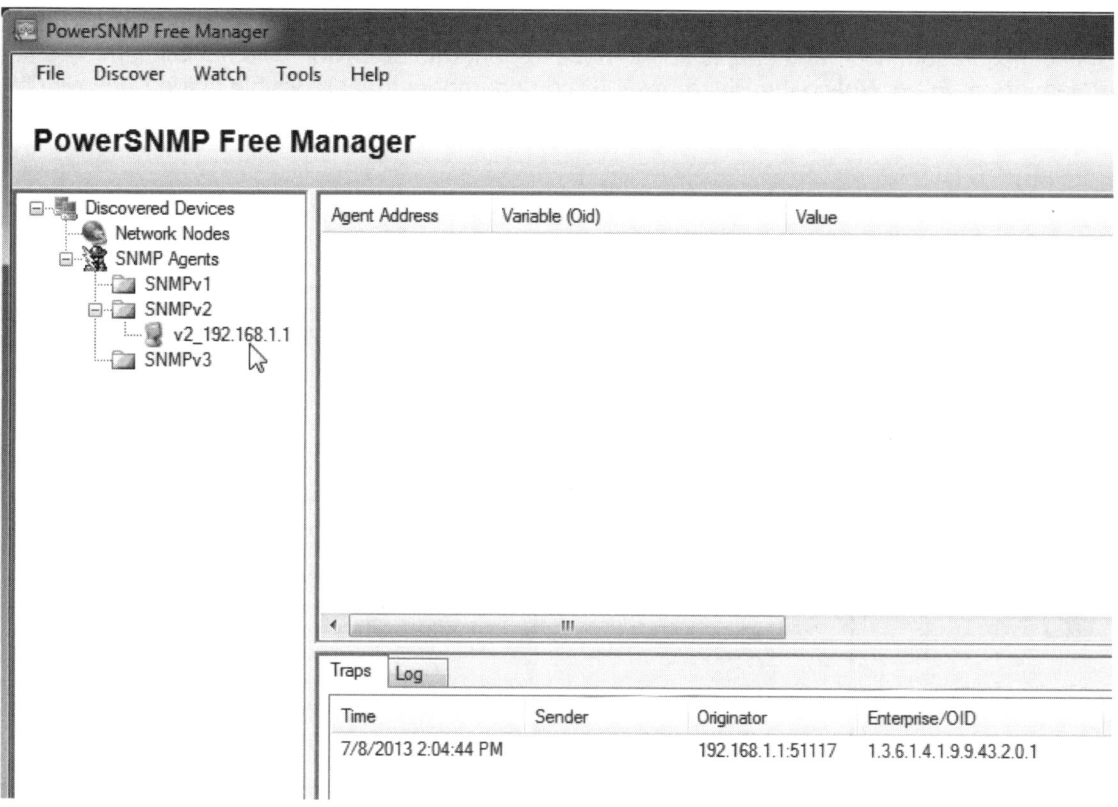


c. Configure S1 as an SNMP agent. You can use the same **snmp-server** commands that you used to configure R1.

d. After S1 is configured, SNMP notifications from 192.168.1.2 display in the Traps window of the PowerSNMP Free Manager. In the PowerSNMP Free Manager, add S1 as an SNMP agent using the same process that you used to discover R1.

## Part 3: Convert OID Codes with the Cisco SNMP Object Navigator

In Part 3, you will force SNMP notifications to be sent to the SNMP manager located at PC-A. You will then convert the received OID codes to names to learn the nature of the messages. The MIB/OID codes can be easily converted using the Cisco SNMP Object Navigator located at http://www.cisco.com.

### Step 1: Clear current SNMP messages.

In the PowerSNMP Free Manager, right-click the **Traps** window and select **Clear** to clear the SNMP messages.

### Step 2: Generate an SNMP trap and notification.

On R1, configure the S0/0/0 interface according to the Addressing Table at the beginning of this lab. Accessing global configuration mode and enable an interface to generate an SNMP trap notification to be sent to the SNMP Manager at PC-A. Notice the Enterprise/OID code numbers that are visible in the traps window.

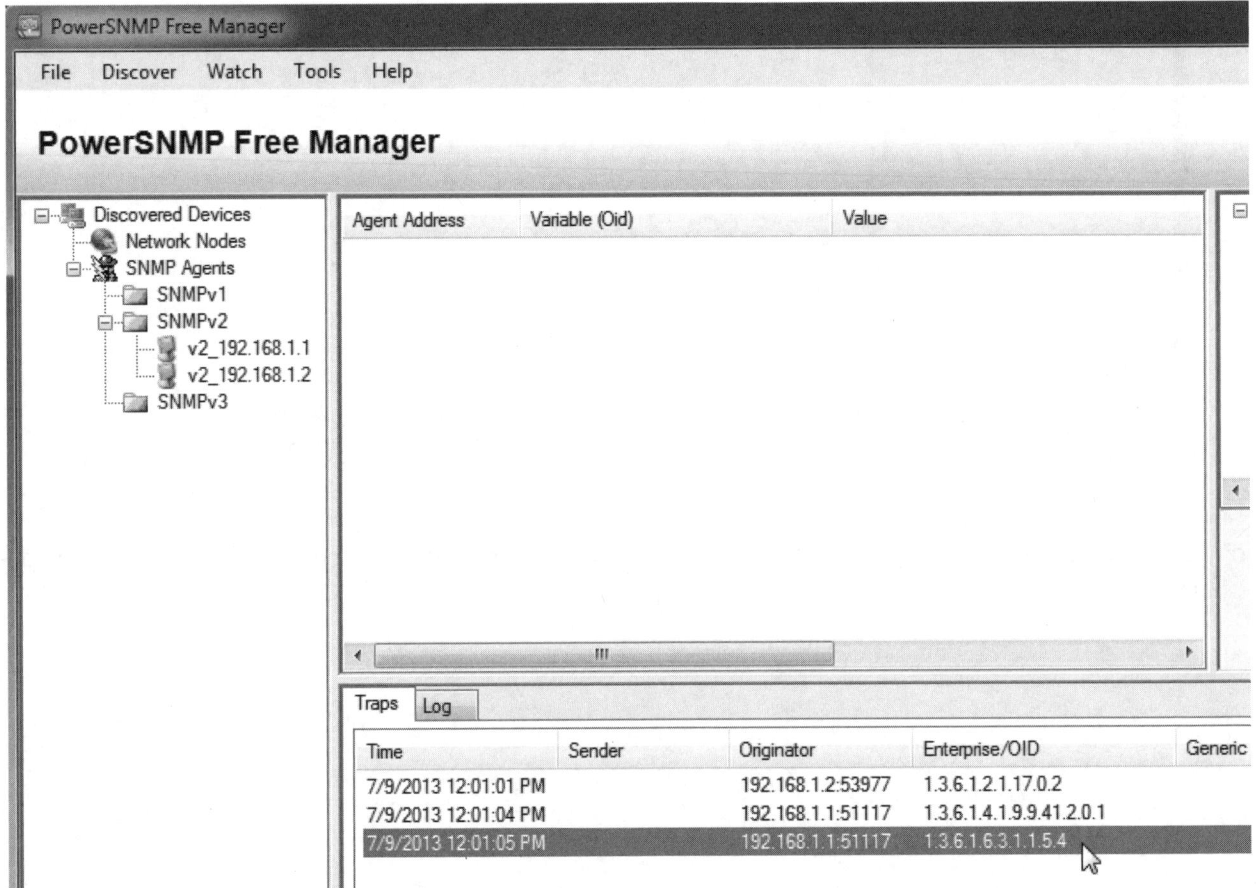


### Step 3: Decode SNMP MIB/OID messages.

From a computer with Internet access, open a web browser and go to http://www.cisco.com.

a. Using the search tool at the top of the window, search for **SNMP Object Navigator**.

b. Choose **SNMP Object Navigator MIB Download MIBs OID OIDs** from the results.

c. Navigate to the **MIB Locator** page. Click the **SNMP Object Navigator**.

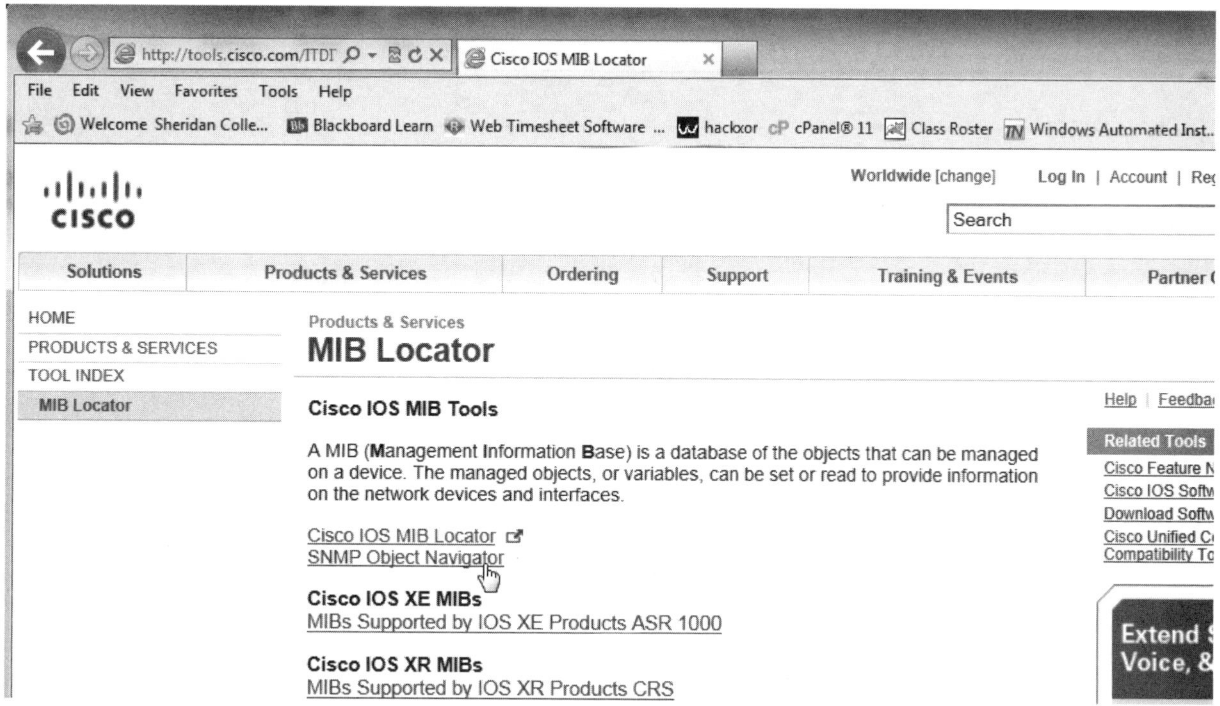


d. Using the **SNMP Object Navigator** page, decode the OID code number from the PowerSNMP Free Manager generated in Part 3, Step 2. Enter the OID code number and click **Translate**.

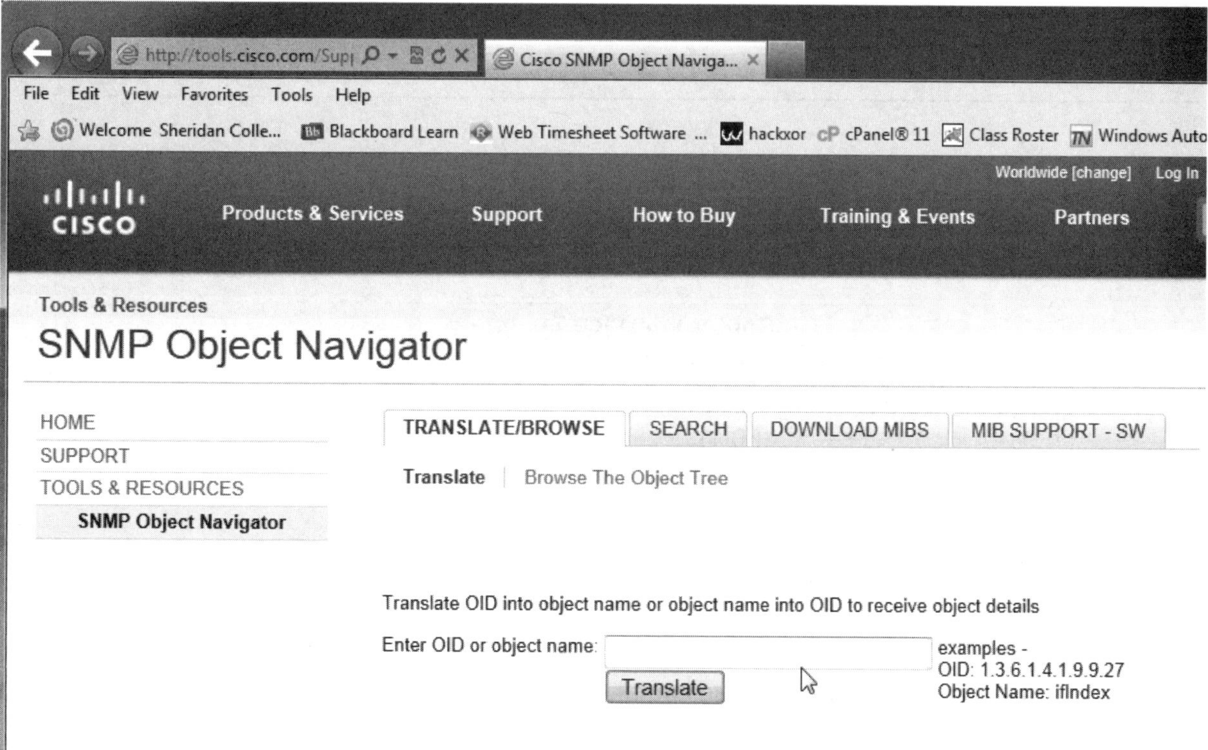

e. Record the OID code numbers and their corresponding message translations below.

______________________________________________________________

______________________________________________________________

______________________________________________________________

______________________________________________________________

______________________________________________________________

## Reflection

1. What are some of the potential benefits of monitoring a network with SNMP?

______________________________________________________________

______________________________________________________________

2. Why is it preferable to solely use read-only access when working with SNMPv2?

______________________________________________________________

______________________________________________________________

## Router Interface Summary Table

| Router Interface Summary | | | | |
|---|---|---|---|---|
| **Router Model** | **Ethernet Interface #1** | **Ethernet Interface #2** | **Serial Interface #1** | **Serial Interface #2** |
| 1800 | Fast Ethernet 0/0 (F0/0) | Fast Ethernet 0/1 (F0/1) | Serial 0/0/0 (S0/0/0) | Serial 0/0/1 (S0/0/1) |
| 1900 | Gigabit Ethernet 0/0 (G0/0) | Gigabit Ethernet 0/1 (G0/1) | Serial 0/0/0 (S0/0/0) | Serial 0/0/1 (S0/0/1) |
| 2801 | Fast Ethernet 0/0 (F0/0) | Fast Ethernet 0/1 (F0/1) | Serial 0/1/0 (S0/1/0) | Serial 0/1/1 (S0/1/1) |
| 2811 | Fast Ethernet 0/0 (F0/0) | Fast Ethernet 0/1 (F0/1) | Serial 0/0/0 (S0/0/0) | Serial 0/0/1 (S0/0/1) |
| 2900 | Gigabit Ethernet 0/0 (G0/0) | Gigabit Ethernet 0/1 (G0/1) | Serial 0/0/0 (S0/0/0) | Serial 0/0/1 (S0/0/1) |

**Note**: To find out how the router is configured, look at the interfaces to identify the type of router and how many interfaces the router has. There is no way to effectively list all the combinations of configurations for each router class. This table includes identifiers for the possible combinations of Ethernet and Serial interfaces in the device. The table does not include any other type of interface, even though a specific router may contain one. An example of this might be an ISDN BRI interface. The string in parenthesis is the legal abbreviation that can be used in Cisco IOS commands to represent the interface.

# 8.3.3.3 Lab – Collecting and Analyzing NetFlow Data

## Topology

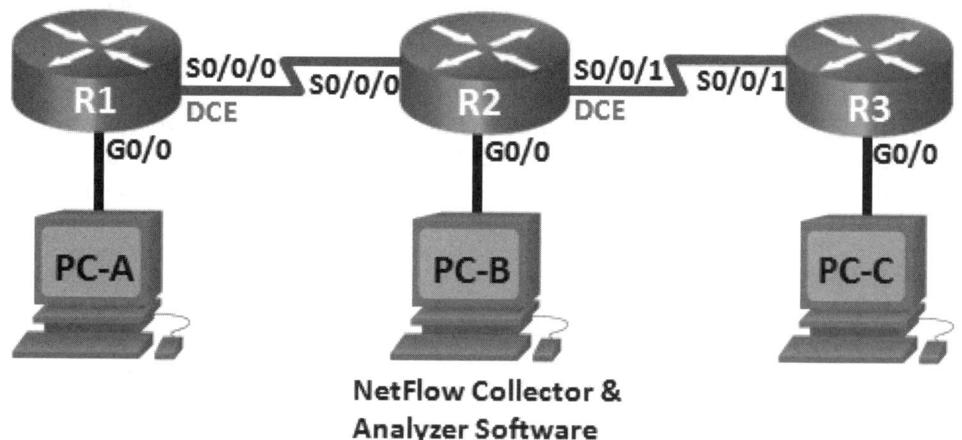


## Addressing Table

| Device | Interface | IP Address | Default Gateway |
|---|---|---|---|
| R1 | G0/0 | 192.168.1.1/24 | N/A |
| | S0/0/0 (DCE) | 192.168.12.1/30 | N/A |
| R2 | G0/0 | 192.168.2.1/24 | N/A |
| | S0/0/0 | 192.168.12.2/30 | N/A |
| | S0/0/1 (DCE) | 192.168.23.1/30 | N/A |
| R3 | G0/0 | 192.168.3.1/24 | N/A |
| | S0/0/1 | 192.168.23.2/30 | N/A |
| PC-A | NIC | 192.168.1.3 | 192.168.1.1 |
| PC-B | NIC | 192.168.2.3 | 192.168.2.1 |
| PC-C | NIC | 192.168.3.3 | 192.168.3.1 |

## Objectives

**Part 1: Build the Network and Configure Basic Device Settings**

**Part 2: Configure NetFlow on a Router**

**Part 3: Analyze NetFlow Using the CLI**

**Part 4: Explore NetFlow Collector and Analyzer Software**

## Background / Scenario

NetFlow is a Cisco IOS technology that provides statistics on packets flowing through a Cisco router or multilayer switch. NetFlow enables network and security monitoring, network planning, traffic analysis, and IP accounting. It is important not to confuse NetFlow's purpose and results with that of packet capture hardware and software. Packet capturing records all possible information exiting or entering a network device for later analysis, NetFlow targets specific statistical information.

Flexible NetFlow is the latest NetFlow technology, improving on the original NetFlow by adding the capability to customize the traffic analysis parameters. Flexible NetFlow uses the Version 9 export format. Starting with Cisco IOS Release 15.1, many useful Flexible NetFlow commands are supported.

In this lab, you will configure NetFlow to capture both ingress (incoming) and egress (outgoing) packets. You will use **show** commands to verify that NetFlow is operational and gathering statistical information. You will also explore available options for NetFlow collection and analysis software.

**Note**: The routers used with CCNA hands-on labs are Cisco 1941 Integrated Services Routers (ISRs) with Cisco IOS Release 15.2(4)M3 (universalk9 image). Other routers and Cisco IOS versions can be used. Depending on the model and Cisco IOS version, the commands available and output produced might vary from what is shown in the labs. Refer to the Router Interface Summary Table at the end of this lab for the correct interface identifiers.

**Note**: Make sure that the routers have been erased and have no startup configurations. If you are unsure, contact your instructor.

## Required Resources

- 3 Routers (Cisco 1941 with Cisco IOS Release 15.2(4)M3 universal image or comparable)
- 3 PCs (Windows 7, Vista, or XP with terminal emulation program, such as Tera Term)
- Console cables to configure the Cisco IOS devices via the console ports
- Ethernet and serial cables as shown in the topology

# Part 1: Build the Network and Configure Basic Device Settings

In Part 1, you will set up the network topology and configure basic settings on the PC hosts and routers.

### Step 1: Cable the network as shown in the topology.

### Step 2: Initialize and reload the routers as necessary.

### Step 3: Configure basic settings for each router.

a. Disable DNS lookup.
b. Configure device names as shown in the topology.
c. Assign **class** as the encrypted privileged EXEC mode password.
d. Assign **cisco** as the console and vty passwords and enable login.
e. Encrypt the plain text passwords.
f. Configure a MOTD banner to warn users that unauthorized access is prohibited.
g. Configure **logging synchronous** for the console line.
h. Set the clock rate for all DCE serial interfaces at **128000**.
i. Configure the IP addresses as listed in the Addressing Table.
j. Configure OSPF using Process ID 1 and advertise all networks. Ethernet interfaces should be passive.
k. Create a local database on R3 with the username **admin** and password **cisco** with the privilege level at **15**.
l. On R3, enable the HTTP service and authenticate HTTP users by using the local database.
m. Copy the running configuration to the startup configuration.

### Step 4: Configure PC hosts.

### Step 5: Verify end-to-end connectivity.

All devices should be able to ping other deices in the topology. Troubleshoot as necessary until end-to-end connectivity is established.

**Note**: It may be necessary to disable the PC firewall for pings between PCs to be successful.

## Part 2: Configure NetFlow on a Router

In Part 2, you will configure NetFlow on router R2. NetFlow will capture all ingress and egress traffic on the R2 serial interfaces and export the data to the NetFlow collector, PC-B. Flexible NetFlow Version 9 will be used to export to the NetFlow collector.

### Step 1: Configure NetFlow capture.

Configure NetFlow data capture on both serial interfaces. Capture data from ingress and egress packets.

```
R2(config)# interface s0/0/0
R2(config-if)# ip flow ingress
R2(config-if)# ip flow egress
R2(config-if)# interface s0/0/1
R2(config-if)# ip flow ingress
R2(config-if)# ip flow egress
```

### Step 2: Configure NetFlow data export.

Use the **ip flow-export destination** command to identify the IP address and the UDP port of the NetFlow collector to which the router should export NetFlow data. UDP Port number 9996 will be used for this configuration.

```
R2(config)# ip flow-export destination 192.168.2.3 9996
```

### Step 3: Configure the NetFlow export version.

Cisco routers running IOS 15.1 support NetFlow versions 1, 5, and 9. Version 9 is the most versatile export data format, but is not backward-compatible with earlier versions. Use the **ip flow-export version** command to set the NetFlow version.

```
R2(config)# ip flow-export version 9
```

### Step 4: Verify the NetFlow configuration.

a. Issue the **show ip flow interface** command to review the NetFlow capture interface information.

```
R2# show ip flow interface
Serial0/0/0
  ip flow ingress
  ip flow egress
Serial0/0/1
  ip flow ingress
  ip flow egress
```

b. Issue the **show ip flow export** command to review the NetFlow data export information.

```
R2# show ip flow export
Flow export v9 is enabled for main cache
```

```
Export source and destination details :
VRF ID : Default
  Destination(1)  192.168.2.3 (9996)
Version 9 flow records
388 flows exported in 63 udp datagrams
0 flows failed due to lack of export packet
0 export packets were sent up to process level
0 export packets were dropped due to no fib
0 export packets were dropped due to adjacency issues
0 export packets were dropped due to fragmentation failures
0 export packets were dropped due to encapsulation fixup failures
```

## Part 3: Analyze NetFlow Using the CLI

In Part 3, you will generate data traffic between R1 and R3 to observe NetFlow technology.

### Step 1: Generate data traffic between R1 and R3.

a. Telnet from R1 to R3 using the IP address 192.168.3.1. Enter the password **cisco** to enter the user EXEC mode. Enter the password **class** to enable global EXEC mode. Issue the **show run** command to generate some Telnet traffic. Keep your Telnet session active for now.

b. From R3, issue the **ping 192.168.1.1 repeat 1000** command to ping the R1 G0/0 interface. This will generate ICMP traffic through R2.

c. From PC-A, browse to R3 using the 192.168.3.1 IP address. Login as **admin** with the password **cisco**. Keep the browser open after you have logged into R3.

   **Note**: Make sure the pop-up blocker is disabled on your browser.

### Step 2: Display a summary of the NetFlow accounting statistics.

On R2, issue the **show ip cache flow** command to display changes to the summary of NetFlow data, including packet size distribution, IP flow information, captured protocols, and interface activity. Notice the protocols now display in the summary data.

```
R2# show ip cache flow
IP packet size distribution (5727 total packets):
   1-32   64   96  128  160  192  224  256  288  320  352  384  416  448  480
   .000 .147 .018 .700 .000 .001 .001 .001 .001 .011 .009 .001 .002 .000 .001

    512  544  576 1024 1536 2048 2560 3072 3584 4096 4608
   .001 .001 .097 .000 .000 .000 .000 .000 .000 .000 .000

IP Flow Switching Cache, 278544 bytes
  2 active, 4094 inactive, 114 added
  1546 ager polls, 0 flow alloc failures
  Active flows timeout in 30 minutes
  Inactive flows timeout in 15 seconds
IP Sub Flow Cache, 34056 bytes
  0 active, 1024 inactive, 112 added, 112 added to flow
  0 alloc failures, 0 force free
  1 chunk, 1 chunk added
  last clearing of statistics 00:07:35
```

```
Protocol         Total     Flows    Packets Bytes  Packets Active(Sec) Idle(Sec)
--------         Flows      /Sec     /Flow  /Pkt     /Sec    /Flow      /Flow
TCP-Telnet           4       0.0        27    43      0.2      5.0       15.7
TCP-WWW            104       0.2        14   275      3.4      2.1        1.5
ICMP                 4       0.0      1000   100      8.8     27.9       15.4

SrcIf          SrcIPaddress    DstIf          DstIPaddress    Pr SrcP DstP  Pkts
Total:              112      0.2         50   146       12.5      3.1         2.5

SrcIf          SrcIPaddress    DstIf          DstIPaddress    Pr SrcP DstP  Pkts
Se0/0/0        192.168.12.1    Null           224.0.0.5       59 0000 0000    43
Se0/0/1        192.168.23.2    Null           224.0.0.5       59 0000 0000    40
```

### Step 3: End the Telnet and browser sessions.

a. Issue the **exit** command on R1 to disconnect from the Telnet session to R3.

b. Close the browser session on PC-A.

### Step 4: Clear NetFlow accounting statistics.

a. On R2, issue the **clear ip flow stats** command to clear NetFlow accounting statistics.

```
R2# clear ip flow stats
```

b. Re-issue the **show ip cache flow** command to verify that the NetFlow accounting statistics have been reset. Notice that, even though you are no longer generating data through R2, data is being picked up by NetFlow. In the example below, the destination address for this traffic is multicast address 224.0.0.5, or OSPF LSA data.

```
R2# show ip cache flow
IP packet size distribution (124 total packets):
   1-32   64   96  128  160  192  224  256  288  320  352  384  416  448  480
   .000 .000 1.00 .000 .000 .000 .000 .000 .000 .000 .000 .000 .000 .000 .000

    512  544  576 1024 1536 2048 2560 3072 3584 4096 4608
   .000 .000 .000 .000 .000 .000 .000 .000 .000 .000 .000

IP Flow Switching Cache, 278544 bytes
  2 active, 4094 inactive, 2 added
  1172 ager polls, 0 flow alloc failures
  Active flows timeout in 30 minutes
  Inactive flows timeout in 15 seconds
IP Sub Flow Cache, 34056 bytes
  2 active, 1022 inactive, 2 added, 2 added to flow
  0 alloc failures, 0 force free
  1 chunk, 0 chunks added
  last clearing of statistics 00:09:48
Protocol         Total     Flows    Packets Bytes  Packets Active(Sec) Idle(Sec)
--------         Flows      /Sec     /Flow  /Pkt     /Sec    /Flow      /Flow
IP-other             2       0.0       193    79      0.6   1794.8        5.7
Total:               2       0.0       193    79      0.6   1794.8        5.7


SrcIf          SrcIPaddress    DstIf          DstIPaddress    Pr SrcP DstP  Pkts
Se0/0/0        192.168.12.1    Null           224.0.0.5       59 0000 0000    35

SrcIf          SrcIPaddress    DstIf          DstIPaddress    Pr SrcP DstP  Pkts
Se0/0/1        192.168.23.2    Null           224.0.0.5       59 0000 0000    33
```

## Part 4: Explore NetFlow Collector and Analyzer Software

NetFlow Collector and Analyzer Software is available from many vendors. Some software is provided as freeware, others are not. The following URL provides a summary web page of some of the Freeware NetFlow software available: http://www.cisco.com/en/US/prod/iosswrel/ps6537/ps6555/ps6601/networking_solutions_products_genericcontent0900aecd805ff72b.html

Review this web page to acquaint yourself with some of the available NetFlow Collector and Analyzer software products.

### Reflection

1. What is the purpose of NetFlow collector software?

_______________________________________________

_______________________________________________

_______________________________________________

2. What is the purpose of NetFlow analyzer software?

_______________________________________________

_______________________________________________

_______________________________________________

3. What are the seven critical fields used by the original NetFlow to distinguish flows?

_______________________________________________

_______________________________________________

## Router Interface Summary Table

| Router Interface Summary | | | | |
|---|---|---|---|---|
| **Router Model** | **Ethernet Interface #1** | **Ethernet Interface #2** | **Serial Interface #1** | **Serial Interface #2** |
| 1800 | Fast Ethernet 0/0 (F0/0) | Fast Ethernet 0/1 (F0/1) | Serial 0/0/0 (S0/0/0) | Serial 0/0/1 (S0/0/1) |
| 1900 | Gigabit Ethernet 0/0 (G0/0) | Gigabit Ethernet 0/1 (G0/1) | Serial 0/0/0 (S0/0/0) | Serial 0/0/1 (S0/0/1) |
| 2801 | Fast Ethernet 0/0 (F0/0) | Fast Ethernet 0/1 (F0/1) | Serial 0/1/0 (S0/1/0) | Serial 0/1/1 (S0/1/1) |
| 2811 | Fast Ethernet 0/0 (F0/0) | Fast Ethernet 0/1 (F0/1) | Serial 0/0/0 (S0/0/0) | Serial 0/0/1 (S0/0/1) |
| 2900 | Gigabit Ethernet 0/0 (G0/0) | Gigabit Ethernet 0/1 (G0/1) | Serial 0/0/0 (S0/0/0) | Serial 0/0/1 (S0/0/1) |
| **Note**: To find out how the router is configured, look at the interfaces to identify the type of router and how many interfaces the router has. There is no way to effectively list all the combinations of configurations for each router class. This table includes identifiers for the possible combinations of Ethernet and Serial interfaces in the device. The table does not include any other type of interface, even though a specific router may contain one. An example of this might be an ISDN BRI interface. The string in parenthesis is the legal abbreviation that can be used in Cisco IOS commands to represent the interface. | | | | |

# 8.4.1.1 Class Activity – A Network Administrator's Toolbox for Monitoring

## Objective

Explain different resources that can be used to receive router log messages.

## Scenario

As the network administrator for a small- to medium-sized business, you have just started using CLI network monitoring on the company routers, switches, and servers.

You decide to create a situational listing explaining when to use each method. Network monitoring methods to include are:

- Syslog
- SNMP
- NetFlow

## Resources

- Word processing software

## Directions

**Step 1: Create several situations where Syslog, SNMP, and Net Flow would be used by a network administrator.**

**Step 2: List the situations in matrix format and ask another student or group to identify which CLI monitoring tool to use to gather information about the network issues described.**

**Step 3: Share the matrix with another group or the class.**

# Chapter 9 — Troubleshooting the Network

## 9.0.1.2 Class Activity – Network Breakdown

### Objective

Troubleshoot IP connectivity using basic commands.

### Scenario

You have just moved in to your new office, and your network is very small. After a long weekend of setting up the new network, you discover that it is not working correctly.

Some of the devices cannot access each other and some cannot access the router which connects to the ISP.

It is your responsibility to troubleshoot and fix the problems. You decide to start with basic commands to identify possible troubleshooting areas.

### Resources

- Packet Tracer software

### Directions

#### Step 1: Create a simple network topology using Packet Tracer software, including:

a. Two connected 1941 series routers

b. Two Cisco 2960 switches, one switch connected to each router to form two LANs

c. Six end-user devices

1) A printer and three PCs or laptops on LAN1

2) Two servers on LAN2

#### Step 2: Configure the network and user devices and verify that everything is working correctly. Make an error or two in the configurations. Be sure to turn off the Options, Preferences, and the Show Link Lights setting available on the Packet Tracer software.

#### Step 3: Share your saved Packet Tracer file with another group – have them find and fix the problems using the following commands only:

- `ping`
- `traceroute`
- `telnet`
- `show interface`
- `show IP interface brief` or `show IPv6 interface brief`
- `show IP route` or `show IPv6 route`
- `show running-config`
- `show protocols`
- `show vlan`

#### Step 4: Share the results of the activity with the class or your instructor. How did the groups fix the problems?

# 9.3.1.1 Class Activity – Documentation Development

## Objective

Using a systematic approach, troubleshoot issues in a small- to medium-sized business network.

## Scenario

As the network administrator for a small business, you want to implement a documentation system to use with troubleshooting network-based problems.

After much thought, you decide to compile simple network documentation information into a file to be used when network problems arise. You also know that if the company gets larger in the future, this file can be used to export the information to a computerized, network software system.

To start the network documentation process, you include:

- A physical diagram of your small business network.
- A logical diagram of your small business network.
- Network configuration information for major devices, including routers and switches.

## Resources

- Packet Tracer software
- Word processing software

**Step 1: Create a Packet Tracer file to simulate a very small business network. Include these devices:**

- One router with at least two Ethernet ports
- Two switches connected to the router (LAN1 and LAN2)
- Five user devices to include PCs, laptops, servers, and printers connected either of the two LANs.

**Step 2: Create a word-processing file in matrix format to record each of the following main network-documentation areas:**

a. Physical topology and information

  1) Type of device and model name

  2) Network hostname

  3) Location of the device

  4) Cable connections types and ports

b. Logical topology information

  1) IOS or OS image versions

  2) IP addresses (IPv4, IPv6, or both)

  3) Data-link addresses (MAC)

  4) VLAN addresses

c. Network device configuration information

  1) Location of backup file (TFTP server, USB, text file)

  2) Text-formatted, configuration script per router and switch devices

**Step 3: Share your Packet Tracer file and network documentation with a classmate, another group, the class, or your Instructor according to the instructions provided. Discuss how this information could be useful to any network administrator.**